Sex Differences and Discrimination in Education

edited by

Scarvia B. Anderson
Educational Testing Service,
Princeton, New Jersey

Charles A. Jones Publishing Company
Worthington, Ohio

©1972 by Wadsworth Publishing Company, Inc., Belmont, California 94002.
All rights reserved. No part of this book may be reproduced, stored in a
retrieval system, or transcribed, in any form or by any means, electronic,
mechanical, photocopying, recording, or otherwise, without the prior
written permission of the publisher, Charles A. Jones Publishing Company,
Worthington, Ohio 43085, a division of Wadsworth Publishing Company,
Inc.

2   3   4   5   6   7   8   9   10   /   76   75   74   73

Library of Congress Catalog Card Number: 72-85892
International Standard Book Number: 0-8396-0027-5

Printed in the United States of America

031103

Contents

Part One: Sex Differences

Chapter

I. What Kind of Difference Does Sex Make? *Samuel Messick*   2

The Nature of Sex Differences, 3
Determinants of Sex Differences, 4
The Future of Sex Differences, 6
    Differences in Values, 7; The Value of Differences, 7

II. Sex Differences in Intellectual Functioning, *Eleanor E. Maccoby*   9

Correlations between Intellectual Performance and
    Personality Characteristics, 11
        Impulse Control, 12; Fearfulness and Anxiety, 12;
        Aggression and Competitiveness, 13; Level of
        Aspiration and Achievement Motivation, 13; Sex-
        Typing, 15; Dependency, Passivity, and
        Independence, 16
Possible Causal Factors of Sex Differences in
    Intellectual Abilities, 16
        Developmental Timetable, 16; Direct Effects of
        Sex-Typed Interests, 17; Opportunities to Learn,
        18; "Identification" and Modeling, 18; Sex-Typed
        Personality Traits as Mediating Processes, 19
Genetic Versus Environmental Contributions, 24

Part Two: Schools and Preschools

III. He Only Does It To Annoy, *Marshall P. Smith*   28

Differences Start at or before Birth, 28
The Girls Are Ready for the School, 30
The School Is the Way the Children See It, 32
Upper Grades—More of the Same, 34
Girls Get the A's But the Boys Grow, 37
What Way Out? 42

IV. "Look, Jane, Look! See Dick Run and Jump! Admire Him!" *Karen DeCrow*   44

Textbook Content and Women, 44
Social Studies Content, 46
Reading about Differences, 47
Women in Literature, 48

V. Are Little Girls Being Harmed by "Sesame Street"? *Jane Bergman*   50

Puppets and Cartoons, 50
Films, 51
"Real" People, 52
Perpetuation of Stereotypes, 53

VI. Down the Up Staircase: Sex Roles, Professionalization, and the Status of Teachers, *Barbara Heyns*   54

Status of Teachers, 55
Historical Background, 55
Sex Roles in Teaching, 56
Salaries, 57
Teacher Organizations, 58
Conclusion, 59

Contributors

Scarvia B. Anderson, executive director for special development, Educational Testing Service

Jane Bergman, writer

T. Anne Cleary, executive director of examinations, College Entrance Examination Board

Margaret M. Clifford, assistant professor of educational psychology, University of Iowa

Karen DeCrow, attorney; eastern regional director of NOW

Barbara Heyns, assistant professor, Graduate School of Education, Harvard University; Center for Educational Policy Research

Eleanor E. Maccoby, professor of psychology, Stanford University

Samuel Messick, vice president, research, Educational Testing Service

David Riesman, Henry Ford II professor of the social sciences, Harvard University; member, Program in Social Sciences 1971-72, The Institute for Advanced Study

Lawrence A. Simpson, director of placement, associate professor of education, University of Virginia

Marshall P. Smith, professor of psychology, Trenton State College

Sheila Tobias, associate provost, Wesleyan University

Ethel Bent Walsh, commissioner, Equal Employment Opportunity Commission

Elaine Walster, professor of sociology, University of Wisconsin

Sex Differences and Discrimination in Education

THE NATIONAL SOCIETY
FOR THE STUDY OF EDUCATION

Series on Contemporary Educational Issues
Kenneth J. Rehage, Series Editor

The 1971 Titles

Accountability in Education, Leon M. Lessinger and Ralph W. Tyler, Editors

Farewell to Schools??? Daniel U. Levine and Robert J. Havighurst, Editors

Models for Integrated Education, Daniel U. Levine, Editor

PYGMALION Reconsidered, Janet D. Elashoff and Richard E. Snow

Reactions to Silberman's CRISIS IN THE CLASSROOM, A. Harry Passow, Editor

The 1972 Titles

Black Students in White Schools, Edgar A. Epps, Editor

Flexibility in School Programs, Willard J. Congreve and George J. Rinehart, Editors

Performance Contracting—1969-1971, James A. Mecklenburger

The Potential of Educational Futures, Michael Marien and Warren L. Ziegler, Editors

Sex Differences and Discrimination in Education, Scarvia Anderson, Editor

The National Society for the Study of Education also publishes Yearbooks which are distributed by the University of Chicago Press.

Inquiries regarding membership in the Society may be addressed to Kenneth J. Rehage, Secretary-Treasurer, 5835 Kimbark Avenue, Chicago 60637.

Preface

I have been pleasantly aware that concern about educational opportunity and employment for women has been mounting rapidly. However, I had not realized that this concern was backed up by quite so many speeches, articles, books, reports, and "pages of testimony." Thus the difficult part of assembling this book for the National Society for the Study of Education was deciding what to put in and what to leave out, and the second decision was even harder than the first.

The selection of materials was necessarily related to the projected length of the book. It was also influenced by the notions that 1) since sex discrimination, bias, stereotyping, or at best thoughtlessness pervade all levels of education, the book should treat all levels to some extent; 2) the book itself should be unbiased at least to the degree that it included writings of both men and women and entertained possible discrimination against males as well as females; 3) since sexual attitudes may be transmitted both directly through educational personnel and indirectly through the materials they write and use, the book should include a section on educational media; 4) considerations of possible sex discrimination in education would be most meaningful in light of some familiarity with the literature of sex differences; and 5) finally, other things being equal, preference should be given to interpretations and conclusions with a "hard data" or empirical base.

For a book so short, assembled in such a short time, the list of those who contribute to it in one way or another is long: Juliette Anderson, Ruth Ekstrom, Eliza Kealy, Connie Kennedy, Rita Poore; the authors and publishers who generously gave permission to reprint and sometimes abridge articles and speeches; and especially my two dear old friends and dear new friend who filled important gaps with the original chapters they produced.

I cannot resist ending this preface and beginning this book with the words of Lady Winchilsea, *c.* 1700:

> Alas! a woman that attempts the pen,
> Such an intruder on the rights of men,
> Such a presumptuous Creature, is esteem'd,
> The fault, can by no vertue by redeem'd.
> They tell us, we mistake our sex and way;
> Good breeding, fassion, dancing, dressing, play
> Are the accomplishments we should desire;
> To write or read, or think, or to enquire
> Would cloud our beauty, and exhaust our time,
> And interrupt the Conquests of our prime.

Scarvia B. Anderson

Series Foreword

Sex Differences and Discrimination in Education is one of a group of five publications constituting the second set in a series prepared under the auspices of the National Society for the Study of Education. Other titles in this second set of paperbacks dealing with "Contemporary Educational Issues" are:

Performance Contracting—1969-1971, by James Mecklenburger

Flexibility in School Programs, edited by Willard J. Congreve and George J. Rinehart

Black Students in White Schools, edited by Edgar G. Epps

The Potential of Educational Futures, edited by Michael Marien and Warren L. Ziegler

The response to the first set of five paperbacks in this series, published in 1971, has been very encouraging. Like their predecessors the current volumes, all dealing with timely and significant issues in education, present a useful background and analysis for those who seek a deeper understanding of some of the critical educational problems of our times.

Dr. Scarvia Anderson has edited this volume on a topic that continues to be a lively one in educational circles as well as in society generally. Her selection of themes for development in this book has been skillfully done. Her choice of contributors has permitted the inclusion of scholarly analyses of previous research, some reports of very relevant research on particular issues, and some exceedingly thoughtful and provocative pieces, some of which appear here for the first time while others have been published previously elsewhere.

The Society wishes to express its appreciation to Dr. Anderson; to her associates at Educational Testing Service, Princeton, New Jersey; and to each of the authors whose essays are included in this significant volume.

Kenneth J. Rehage
for the Committee on the Expanded Publication
Program of the National Society for the Study of Education

Part Three: Higher Education

VII. Some Dilemmas of Women's Education, *David Riesman*   62

Minority Status, 62
    Solidarity Among Women, 64
The "Male" Mode, 64
    Reactions to the "Male" Models, 66
Women, Careers, and Marriage, 67
What Educational Institutions Can Do, 68
Security for the Men, 70
Still a Man's World, 71
Women in Science, 72
A Look at Other Societies, 72

VIII. The Effect of <u>Race</u> and <u>Sex</u> on College Admission, *Elaine Walster, T. Anne Cleary, and Margaret M. Clifford*   74

Procedure, 75
Independent Variables, 75
Dependent Variables, 77
Results, 78
Analysis of Additional Variables, 80

IX. Coeducation   81

X. How Coeducation Fails Women, *Sheila Tobias*   83

Fear of Success, 85
Passivity and Dependence, 86
Inferiority, 87
Countering the Culture, 88
Women's Studies, 89

XI. A Myth Is Better Than a Miss: Men Get the Edge in Academic Employment, *Lawrence A. Simpson*   92

XII.   Women in Universities, *Ethel Bent Walsh*   96

Discrimination in Admissions, 97
Discrimination in Employment, 99
The Role of Government, 101

XIII. Comment: "Education's and Not Nature's Fools,"
Scarvia B. Anderson
                                                                  103

References   106

Part One

Sex Differences

I am ignorant of any one quality that is amiable in a man which is not equally so in a woman. I do not except even modesty and gentleness of nature. Nor do I know one vice or folly which is not equally detestable in both.

Jonathan Swift
"A Letter to a Very Young
Lady on Her Marriage"
1727

What Kind
of Difference
Does Sex Make?

Samuel Messick

Males and females differ in a variety of ways in their abilities, interests, and personalities. At the same time, there are also noticeable differences in privilege, reward, and status that society affords the two sexes in their typical adult role functioning. Given the juxtaposition of these two points, it is tempting to seize upon the very existence of sex differences as evidence of sex discrimination and to presume that the early and systematic induction of these differences is somehow instrumental to the production and maintenance of subsequent inequities. If this were so, then rhetoric calling for a blurring of sex differences would not be just a symbol in the battle for equality of the sexes but a calculated strategy for accomplishing the desired end. But such a strategy depends heavily upon an instrumental link between the emergence of sex differences and the subsequent occurrence of discrimination, when the opposite sequence might be the case instead—one, that is, in which sex differences derive from, rather than elicit, discriminatory practices. Both tendencies might be operating together, of course, in iterative and cumulative fashion, but there might also be a genuine independence of the two phenomena.

It is important to recognize that sex differences do not automatically entail sex discrimination and that action programs, such as systematic attempts to modify sex-typed educational and socialization experiences, may have social consequences that go beyond a redressing of sexual inequities. Proposals for extensive changes in the upbringing of boys and girls should take into account the nature and origin of sex differences as well as their determinants and should consider in what direction personality or behavioral changes should occur and in the service of what social values. Should boys be changed to be more like girls? Or girls more like boys? Or both more like the middle ground or like some new ideal? And who is to decide? Let us briefly consider some of these issues.

The Nature of Sex Differences

Research evidence documenting the nature of sex differences in abilities, interests, and personality has been summarized in several recent reviews (2; 88; 149; 154)* one of which is reprinted in abridged form as the next chapter in this book. (92)   In regard to ability differences, males have been generally found to excel in speed and coordination of gross bodily movements, mechanical comprehension, spatial orientation, analytical ability, and quantitative reasoning; whereas females tend to excel in perceptual speed and accuracy, manual dexterity, memory, numerical computation, verbal fluency, and such mechanics of language as grammar and spelling. Females consistently excel in academic achievement throughout the school years but are then substantially outshone by males in almost all aspects of occupational and career achievement. Women are also more predictable academically than men in that their school performance is more nearly in accord with their pattern of abilities and skills, whereas male performance is more variable largely as a function of interests. (132; 141; 142)

Although all of these ability differences are statistically significant, it is difficult to establish which of them are of substantial magnitude, primarily because the size of some of the observed differences may be more reflective of the measurement scale used and of differential experiences with test content than of any basic sex differences in underlying cognitive functioning. This is partly a problem of unknown comparability of units throughout the measurement scale, but partly also a concern that observed score differences might not reflect uniform sex differences in facility but rather differential experience and motivation. Such issues of interpretation are particularly serious when different types of items and item content are used on a test. For example, an apparent sex difference in "verbal ability" favoring males might be reinterpreted if it were seen to be a function of the relative preponderance on the total test of vocabulary items related to "people," which tend to be easier for females, as opposed to items related to "things," which tend to be easier for males. (23)

Even with these caveats in mind, however, it does appear that sex differences in spatial orientation and analytical ability are substantial from the primary grades on (162) and that differences in quantitative

---

*Numbers in parentheses pertain to the preceding material and refer to the References section starting on page 106.

reasoning are substantial by high school age.(5)   On all of these dimensions, however, the mean differences between the sexes are relatively small compared to the enormous variability within sex, which results in a considerable overlap in the distributions of scores for males and females.

Among the major personality differences noted between the sexes are greater aggressiveness, achievement motivation, and emotional stability in the male and a heightened social orientation in the female. General sex differences in passivity, dependency, and activity level—long thought to be consistent and substantial—have recently been called into question.(95)   As with ability variables, there are wide individual differences on these personality dimensions within each sex and a considerable overlap in the distributions of scores for males and females. There is some evidence suggesting that average sex differences are somewhat greater for these personality dimensions than for abilities and that they emerge somewhat earlier. Such generalizations, however, are particularly tenuous because of marked differences in the methods of measurement in the two domains.

Most of the evidence seems to indicate that the largest and most pervasive differences between the sexes are in their interests, values, and general orientation to life. In our society men tend on the average to be more interested in scientific, mechanical, political, computational, and physically strenuous or adventuresome activities, while women tend to prefer literary, musical, artistic, social service, and sedentary activities. In studies of values, men score significantly higher on theoretical, economic, and political values and women on aesthetic, social, and religious values. Comparisons of the interests of American and English children (153) and of the reading interests of American and Finnish children (50) suggest that sex differences in these regards are greater even than nationality differences, at least within this narrow variation of traditional Western culture. But, as with other dimensions of consistent sex differences, there are wide individual differences within each sex and a marked overlap in the distributions of scores for males and females.

The important repetitive element running through this brief summary of psychological sex differences is that individual differences within each sex are far greater than average differences between the sexes and that the distributions of scores for males and females overlap to a striking degree. Hence an individual's sex is an extremely unreliable indicator of his status on most psychological dimensions, and for any important practical purpose there should be concern with measures of individual differences, not sex differences.

Determinants of Sex Differences

It is likely that sex differences in abilities, interests, and personality emerge from a confluence of biological and cultural factors interacting in complex ways. Some of the biological differences that might be influential include sex differences in reproductive functions, hormones, chromosomes, body build and other anatomical features, physiological functioning, and biochemical processes. These physical differences may function directly in shaping sex differences in activities, interests, and achievements in various fields and indirectly by influencing body image and self-concept, which might then serve to mediate a variety of psychological processes. Another possible biological basis for psychological sex differences may be found in the accelerated developmental timetable of girls, which leads them to develop language skills and certain cognitive abilities earlier than boys. There is also some indication of a partial biological underpinning for the pervasive difference in aggressiveness between males and females. (95)   The operation of such biological contributions, however, should not be taken to mean that the psychological variables in question would be unresponsive to cultural influences or social intervention.

The impact of sociocultural influences upon the development of psychological sex differences is undoubtedly massive, with blatant and subtle sex-role distinctions occurring throughout the socialization process. These distinctions find expression through virtually all of the basic mechanisms of socialization, such as the principles of social learning (including not only discrimination learning, generalization, and observational learning or imitation but also the patterning of rewards, nonrewards, and punishments under differential contingencies and the principles of direct and vicarious conditioning); the possibly more subtle process of identification, which implies an internalization of attitudes and values; and the cognitive-developmental evolution of sex-typing. (109; 113) This latter process is a potentially powerful theoretical addition to conceptualizations of social development, for it emphasizes a pervasive organizing function of sexual self-concepts.(86)   In this view, the very early sex labeling of the child leads to a self-schema that assimilates sex-typed interests and values in the service of developing a consistent cognitive organization of social role concepts around universal, perceived sex differences in bodily structure and capacities. The activities of like-sex models are then seen as being more consistent with this self-view, are more interesting and valuable by virtue of this egocentric relation to the self, and hence are more likely to be modeled. Thus, in this theory, sex-typing is not conceived as a product of identification or modeling, but rather identification is seen as a consequence of sex-typing.

Although there is some controversy over the relative causal roles of cognitive self-concepts versus social-learning principles as determinants of personality, (109) there is general consensus that many psychological sex differences, since they are largely attributable in complex ways to sociocultural practices, would be at least partially responsive to changes in those practices. But to be effective these changes in practice may have to be quite complicated, for the causal network of social determinants of sex differences is frequently intricate indeed. E. E. Maccoby, for example, suggests that certain critical sex differences in intellectual functioning may derive from prior differences in sex-typed personality traits that mediate intellectual growth. (92) These mediating processes, furthermore, may sometimes facilitate or inhibit intellectual development for one sex and not the other by virtue of differences in the average position of males and females on mediating dimensions bearing a curvilinear relationship to intellectual performance. If this is the case, then direct attempts to modify sex differences in intellectual functioning may prove futile, while changes in upbringing that affect certain central personality characteristics may have far-reaching intellectual consequences. Given this intricate interrelatedness of human functioning, advocates of change (and, for that matter, advocates of the status quo) should mark well that socialization practices ostensibly pointed toward the shaping of one aspect of the developing organism may bear important and unanticipated ramifications for other aspects of the organism.

With these caveats in view, the basic questions loom even larger. Should extensive changes be fostered in the pattern of psychological sex differences? And if so, in what direction and to what end? And who should decide?

The Future of Sex Differences

One popular response to the emergence of sex differences is to view them as natural to a pervasive biocultural order and to cherish them. An attempt is then made to take proper account of them in educational practice and sometimes even to build upon them to optimize subsequent learning and development, as in segregating the sexes during the primary grades to capitalize pedagogically upon the different developmental timetables of boys and girls or in programming home economics and shop classes along sex lines in junior high school to capitalize upon masculine and feminine interests. However, these and many other educational practices may serve, albeit often unintentionally, to perpetuate and crystallize what initially may have been fairly pliant distinctions between the sexes, thereby contributing additional impetus to what gives every appearance of being a giant social plan to create sex-based stereotypes of adult role functioning. But stereotypes, regardless of their origins, are restrictive—they entail obvious and subtle pressures assimilating the individual to some standardized conception of the group and hence inherently limit individual freedom.

Differences in Values

The social foundations bearing upon what kind of person a little boy or a little girl is to become involve value decisions ordinarily considered, at least at the outset, to be the province of the parent. But the social foundations bearing upon sex-role differentiation implicate so many social forces beyond the parents' ken—in peer groups, in the mass media, in school and preschool programs—that the masculinization of sons and the feminization of daughters can hardly be considered to be under the direct control of pluralistic parental values. The problem is that these processes may not be under the control of any individuals, but rather operate inexorably in some conglomerate fashion in the service of maintaining the existing social system. The educational problem here is that the social system, with its pervasive network of educational and group supports, pressures the individual to conform to sex-role stereotypes, while at the same time the educational system, at least in rhetoric, strives in the name of freedom and pluralism to enhance individual self-determination and to foster diversity. The antithetical elements in this situation cry out for rectification for the good of both society and the individual. One possibility is to consider the uses of education for expanding in meaningful ways the individual's role options, including sex-role options.

The Value of Differences

At this point, the problem does not seem to be sex differences but rather sex stereotypes. The concern is not so much with the fact that the sexes differ on a variety of intellectual and personality dimensions, for those differences were never deemed very large in light of the enormous variation within sex on these dimensions and the marked overlap in the distributions of males and females. Rather, the concern seems to stem from hangups in connection with the overlap. On these sex-typed dimensions, the full range of individual differences, elsewhere so highly prized in the name of diversity, is here viewed with disdain. A girl exhibiting consistently high aggressiveness is considered too "masculine," for example, and a boy displaying intense poetic and literary interests far too "feminine."

One direction for education to follow when faced with such outliers, indeed a direction it may already customarily pursue, is to provide compensatory experiences to these individuals to make them more conformable to sex-role requirements. But there are alternatives. And one of them is to attempt to open up the stereotype to an appreciation of the worth of such cross-sex extremes in human functioning, to free the individual from a bind that pits personal bent against social expectations. One approach to this end would be to present in systematic fashion, from the earliest school experiences on, the full range of role alternatives as realistic possibilities for both sexes, keeping the options open as long as possible so that this most critical aspect of living might come to be a matter of meaningfully informed individual choice.

Thus this chapter fittingly closes with a slight variant of the opening question, similar in form but profoundly different in substance:

What kind of difference should sex make?

II

Sex Differences
in Intellectual Functioning

Eleanor E. Maccoby

. . . Several detailed reviews of the differences between the sexes in average performance on tests of abilities are available in the literature (2; 149). . . . The primary conclusions to be drawn from them are:

1) *General intelligence* Most widely used tests of general intelligence have been standardized to minimize or eliminate sex differences. Whether differences are found on any particular test will depend on the balance of the items—whether there are more items of a kind on which one sex normally excels. There is a tendency for girls to test somewhat higher on tests of general intelligence during the preschool years, boys during the high school years. There is a possibility that the latter finding is in part a function of differential school dropout rates; more boys drop out, leaving a more highly selected group of boys in high school. But some longitudinal studies in which the same children have been tested repeatedly through their growth cycle show greater gains for boys than girls. L. W. Sontag et al., (140) and E. Ebert and K. Simmons (40) both report this finding; N. Bayley (8; 9) does not. The changes in tested intelligence that occur during late adolescence and adulthood appear to favor men somewhat; that is, women decline somewhat more, or gain somewhat less, depending on the test used. (10; 16; 61; 148)

2) *Verbal ability* Through the preschool years and in the early

Abridged from "Sex Differences in Intellectual Functioning," by Eleanor E. Maccoby, from *The Development of Sex Differences* edited by Eleanor E. Maccoby with the permission of the publishers, Stanford University Press. ©1966 by the Board of Trustees of the Leland Stanford Junior University.

school years, girls exceed boys in most aspects of verbal performance. They say their first word sooner, articulate more clearly and at an earlier age, use longer sentences, and are more fluent. By the beginning of school, however, there are no longer any consistent differences in vocabulary. Girls learn to read sooner, and there are more boys than girls who require special training in remedial reading programs; but by approximately the age of ten, a number of studies show that boys have caught up in their reading skills. Throughout the school years, girls do better on tests of grammar, spelling, and word fluency.

3) *Number ability*   Girls learn to count at an earlier age. Through the school years, there are no consistent sex differences in skill at arithmetical computation. During grade school years, some studies show boys beginning to forge ahead on tests of "arithmetical reasoning," although a number of studies reveal no sex differences on this dimension at this time. Fairly consistently, however, boys excel at arithmetical reasoning in high school, and the differences in mathematical skills are substantially in favor of men among college students and adults. In a longitudinal sample, N. Haan finds men accelerating more than women in arithmetical ability during early adulthood. (61)

4) *Spatial ability*   While very young boys and girls do not differ on spatial tasks such as form boards and block design, by the early school years boys consistently do better on spatial tasks, and this difference continues through the high school and college years.

5) *Analytic ability*   This term has several meanings. It is used to refer to the ability to respond to one aspect of a stimulus situation without being greatly influenced by the background or field in which it is presented. In this sense, it is equivalent to what H. A. Witkin calls "field independence." On measures of this trait, such as the Embedded Figures Test and the Rod and Frame Test, boys of school age score consistently and substantially higher than girls.(164)   I. Sigel et al., however, did not find sex differences on an embedded-figures test among a sample of five-year-olds, (136) nor did Maccoby et al., among four-year-olds. (93)

A related meaning of "analytic ability" is concerned with modes of grouping diverse arrays of objects or pictures. People who group "analytically"—put objects together on the basis of some selected element they have in common (e.g., all the persons who have a hand raised)—have been shown to be less influenced by background conditions in recognition tests, and hence are analytic in the Witkin sense as well. Boys more commonly use analytic groupings than do girls. How early this difference emerges is still an open question. Sigel did not find sex differences in grouping behavior among four- and five-year-olds. J. Kagan et al. did find clear sex differences among children in the second to fourth grade. (80)

6) *"Creativity"* There are relatively few studies comparing the sexes on aspects of creativity, and the outcome depends on the definition of the term. If the emphasis is on the ability to break set or restructure a problem, there is a tendency for boys and men to be superior, particularly if the problem involves a large perceptual component. Breaking set is involved in the tasks used to measure "analytic ability," discussed above, and in some of the tests that have a high loading on the space factor.

If creativity is thought of in terms of divergent, as distinct from convergent, thinking, (60) the evidence appears to favor girls somewhat, although the findings are not consistent. A task requiring children to think of ways in which toys could be improved showed that in the first two grades of school, each sex was superior when dealing with toys appropriate to its own sex, but by the third grade, boys were superior on both feminine and masculine toys. On the other hand, girls and women do better on a battery of divergent tasks measuring the variety of ideas produced for the solution of verbally presented problems. (85; 151)

7) *Achievement* Girls get better grades than boys throughout the school years, even in subjects in which boys score higher on standard achievement tests. In adulthood, after graduation from school, men achieve substantially more than women in almost any aspect of intellectual activity where achievements can be compared—books and articles written, artistic productivity, and scientific achievements. A follow-up study of gifted children showed that while gifted boys tended to realize their potential in their occupations and creative output, gifted girls did not.

How large are the group differences summarized above? It is difficult to find a satisfactory answer to this question, for some studies report that a difference between the sexes is statistically significant, without giving the actual magnitude of the mean scores that are being compared. Even when mean scores are given, there is a problem of the meaning of the units on the scale—whether they are equal throughout the scale. With these reservations in mind, existing information does suggest that sex differences in spatial ability and in some aspects of analytic ability are substantial from the early school years on, and that sex differences in mathematical reasoning by high school age are also substantial, while differences in verbal ability are less marked. But on all measures reported, there is considerable overlap between the distribution of scores of the two sexes.

Correlations Between Intellectual Performance and Personality Characteristics

So far, we have been summarizing the known differences between the sexes in their average performance on a variety of tasks. But this, of course, does not provide a complete account of sex differences. Even on tests where the distribution of scores is the same for the two sexes . . . the array of scores will often correlate differently with other variables for boys and girls. . . . (135)

Impulse Control

For the present, we will use the term "impulse" to designate high levels of undirected activity and the inability to delay or inhibit behavior that is incompatible with goal-directed activity. We assume that the ability to persist at a task involves inhibition of competing response tendencies, hence we include both "distractibility" and low task persistence as indicating lack of impulse control.

Sigel et al. report a study of children four to five years old, in which observational measures were taken of 1) emotional control, 2) cautiousness, and 3) attentiveness. (136) In addition, each child was given a grouping test, in which he had to select from an array of pictures the one that was most like a standard. Some children adopted a "descriptive part-whole" grouping style (called analytic responses by Kagan et al. [80]). The sexes did not differ on Sigel's three measures of impulsiveness. But for boys, the frequency of analytic grouping was positively correlated with emotional control, cautiousness, and attentiveness, while for girls these correlations were negative. That is, the girl who used this grouping style was impulsive, the boy controlled. . . .

Kagan and H. A. Moss, in their longitudinal study done at the Fels Institute, report that measures of hyperkinesis (high levels of undirected activity) during childhood correlate negatively with adult intellectual interests for men, while the correlation is slightly positive for women. (79) It appears, then, that impulsiveness may be a negative factor for at least some aspects of intellectual development in boys, but for girls it is a less negative—and perhaps even a positive—factor.

Fearfulness and Anxiety

The Kagan and Moss study also dealt with the relationship between fearfulness and intellectual development. Boys who were timid and cautious in early childhood had higher I.Q.'s and developed greater intellectual interests in adulthood; for girls, the correlations between fearfulness and measures of intellectual performance were zero or negative. . . . Bayley and E. S. Schaefer working with a different longitudinal sample, find timidity and reserve to be negative factors for both sexes, but especially so for boys during middle childhood and adolescence.(11)   The correlations they report between I.Q. and absence of shyness in earlier childhood, however, are more positive for girls than for boys, and hence more consistent with the Kagan and Moss findings. It may be that the relationship between timidity and intellectual performance is highly age-specific, and more so for boys than for girls.

Correlations between measures of anxiety and measures of aptitude or achievement are substantially negative for girls and women, while the correlations are either low negative, zero, or positive for boys and men. The evidence fairly consistently points to this difference in the role anxiety plays for the two sexes, (34; 73; 129; 158) although there is one set of contrary findings. (48)

Aggression and Competitiveness

In one study, aggressiveness, as measured by a peer-nomination technique in classrooms of fifth-grade children, was negatively related (slightly but significantly, r = -.27) to a measure of total intelligence (PMA) for boys, and unrelated to this measure for girls. (96) And in the same study, anxiety over aggression was positively related to intelligence for boys (r = .39), unrelated for girls. In the Fels sample Moss and Kagan found nonphysical aggression was positively related to I. Q. among girls, unrelated among boys. (111) E. K. Beller found, in a sample of five- and six-year-old children, a strong negative relationship between aggressiveness and performance on an embedded-figures test for boys, while these variables were uncorrelated for girls. . . . (12) Thus aggressiveness appears to be more of an inhibitor, or less of a facilitator, for intellectual development among boys than among girls.

In the Fels sample, competitiveness was found to correlate with I.Q., and with progressive increases in I.Q., for both sexes, but the correlations are higher for girls than boys. (111; 140)

Level of Aspiration and Achievement Motivation

The evidence is not clear whether boys or girls have a higher correlation between ability (as measured by I.Q. tests) and achievement. B. N. Phillips et al., working with seventh-grade children, found the correlation to be higher for boys. (118) J. S. Coleman reports that among high school students, boys named as "best scholar" had higher I.Q. scores than girls so named, despite the fact that the girls had higher average I.Q. scores in the population studied. (24) He suggests that girls of this age are caught up in a "double bind." They wish to conform to their parents' and teachers' expectations of good academic performance, but fear that high academic achievement will make them unpopular with boys. As a result of these dual pressures, Coleman suggests, the brightest girls do creditably in school but less than their best. On the other hand, the brightest boys feel free to excel in scholarship and do so in fact.

L. M. Terman and M. H. Oden's follow-up study of gifted children disclosed that, for girls, there was no relationship between the level of occupational achievement and I.Q. as measured during the school years, while for boys this correlation was substantial. (148) There is evidence that girls who are underachievers in high school usually begin to be so at about the onset of puberty, (134) while for boys underachievement in high school usually has an earlier onset. . . .

While additional studies contrasting age levels are needed to confirm the point, it appears that the social pressures to do well or poorly in school may have a reverse time sequence for the two sexes. As noted above, the pressures on bright girls not to do as well as they can tend to be augmented in adolescence, so that correlations between ability and achievement ought to be higher during the early school years. By contrast, peer-group pressures on boys in the early school years are often (though not always) in the direction of achievement in sports and other nonacademic pursuits; and boys of this age are frequently engaged in efforts to achieve autonomy, especially in relation to their mothers, with the result that they are less willing than girls to accede to the demands of their predominantly female teachers. [See Chapter III in this book.] In adolescence, however, especially for middle-class boys, the pressures for college entrance and professional preparation begin to be felt, with the result that the more intelligent boys begin to buckle down at this time. Even in high school, however, the boys' more autonomous approach to their school work is indicated in the greater selectivity of their efforts: boys are likely to do well in subjects that interest them and poorly in subjects that bore them, while girls tend to perform uniformly in all their school subjects. (24)

One factor that may operate to produce a higher correlation between aptitude and performance for boys throughout the school years is that boys appear to evaluate their own abilities and performance more realistically than girls. V. J. Crandall et al. asked children how well they expected to do on a new task they were about to undertake. (29) Among boys, the brighter the boy, the better he expected to do on the new task ($r = .62$). Among girls, the brighter the girl the *less* well she expected to do on a new task ($r = -.41$). Furthermore, when the children were asked whether they believed that their score on a task was mostly a function of their own efforts, or a matter of chance or luck, the brighter boys more often believed that success was an outcome of their own efforts. Among the girls, there was no relationship between I.Q. and belief in self-responsibility versus chance. . . .

There is some evidence that girls appear to be more afraid of failure, and more disorganized by it, than boys. M. G. Harmatz, working with college students, found that when women were working on a fairly difficult task and were told that they were not doing well on it, both their level of aspiration and their performance declined, as compared with a control group of women who did not receive this negative feedback. (64) This is consistent with D. McClelland's finding that among women the level of achievement motivation (as reflected in TAT stories) is not affected by an "arousal" treatment involving academic competition, while among men it is increased . . . . (101)

Sex-Typing

"Masculinity" and "Femininity" have been measured in a number of ways. Some of the standard measures have a single scale running from masculine to feminine. Others measure masculinity and femininity independently, so that it is possible for an individual to obtain a high score on both measures if he possesses traits commonly labeled as characteristic of the two different sexes.(17; 116) Using the latter kind of measure, R. Oetzel found that, among fifth-grade boys, total PMA scores were positively correlated with femininity and slightly negatively correlated with masculinity; in other words, the brighter boys were considerably more feminine and slightly less masculine than their less intelligent peers. (116) Among girls, however, total PMA scores were slightly positively correlated with both masculinity and femininity. This means that the high I.Q. girl is likely to be dominant and striving (characteristics labeled "masculine"), but she may also act more "grown-up" and be more anxious to do things for other people than her less intelligent peers (behaviors normally classified as "feminine").

Oetzel's study investigated sex-typing among groups of eleven-year-old children with uneven profiles of abilities, and she found that the children who were more skillful at spatial tasks than verbal or numerical tasks tended to be low in masculinity if they were boys, high in masculinity if they were girls. This trend was confirmed (significantly for boys) in a study with the Fels longitudinal sample . . . . (94)

Both F. Barron and D. W. MacKinnon report that men who are outstanding in originality or creativity score more toward the feminine end of an M-F scale than do their less creative counterparts. (7;97) This difference, they say, reflects a greater breadth of interests among creative men; for example, such men have aesthetic interests, which are usually included as feminine indicators on an M-F scale because women are, on the average, more likely than men to have strong aesthetic interests. . . .

The studies cited so far indicate that analytic thinking, creativity, and high general intelligence are associated with cross-sex-typing, in that the men and boys who score high are more feminine, and the women and girls more masculine, than their low-scoring same-sex counterparts. . . . It is important to note, however, that this cross-sex-typing does not imply that intellectual individuals are sexually uninterested in, or unattractive to, the opposite sex. It merely means that they share more of the interests and activities normally characteristic of the opposite sex.

Dependency,
Passivity, and Independence

For both sexes, there is a tendency for the more passive-dependent children to perform poorly on a variety of intellectual tasks, and for independent children to excel. However, for some kinds of tasks, the relationships are stronger for boys than for girls, and for others the reverse is true. In the Fels longitudinal study, observational measures of dependency were taken, and were then related to I.Q. (111) For boys, the correlations ranged from zero to slightly positive. For girls, they were negative; that is, the less dependent girls were the brighter ones.

Also using the Fels sample, Sontag et al., studied the personality factors associated with progressive increases in I.Q., and found that independence was a factor for both sexes, but that the relationship was considerably stronger for boys. . . . (140)

Possible Causal Factors of Sex Differences in Intellectual Abilities

The research summarized so far has shown that 1) there are a number of aspects of intellectual performance on which the sexes differ consistently in the average scores obtained, and that 2) whether or not there is a difference in average performance on a given task, there are some substantial sex differences in the intercorrelations between intellectual performance and other characteristics of the individual. . . . We turn now to an examination of several possible explanations for these differences.

Developmental Timetable

Physiologically, girls mature faster than boys. And because certain aspects of intellectual development cannot occur until the relevant physical structures are complete, we might expect girls to develop some abilities earlier than boys. For example, at birth the cortical structures relevant to speech are not fully formed. Insofar as speech must wait until they are, we might expect girls to talk sooner than boys. The physiological timetable, of course, determines not only the individual's rate of development in early life but also the age at which he reaches his optimum level, the duration of his stay at this level, and the time of onset and the rate of the aging process. The fact that females mature faster during the first part of the life cycle does not necessarily imply that they begin to age sooner, although they may, despite their greater average longevity.

The sex differences found in general intelligence during the early part of the life span, insofar as these differences may be determined from tests standardized to minimize them, do seem to parallel the physiological trends. But Bayley has shown that the rate of intellectual growth is unrelated to the rate of physical growth if one scores both in terms of the percent of mature growth attained. (8) Hence it does not appear that there is any single developmental timetable controlling both physical and mental growth. In any case, even if some of the differences could be accounted for in terms of different developmental timetables, it is doubtful whether some of the major differences we have noted could be so explained. It is difficult to see, for example, why maturational factors should produce greater differences between the sexes in spatial than verbal performance. We must therefore turn to different explanatory concepts.

Direct Effects of Sex-Typed Interests

Perhaps the explanation for the differences we have noted is very simple: members of each sex are encouraged in, and become interested in and proficient at, the kinds of tasks that are most relevant to the roles they fill currently or are expected to fill in the future. According to this view, boys in high school forge ahead in math because they and their parents and teachers know they may become engineers or scientists; on the other hand, girls know that they are unlikely to need math in the occupations they will take up when they leave school. And adult women, most of whom become housewives or work at jobs that do not make many intellectual demands, decline in measures of "total intelligence" because such tests call upon skills that are not being used by adult women as extensively as they are used by adult men. As far as women's lack of creativity and intellectual productivity is concerned, we could argue that women are busy managing households and rearing children; and that these activities usually preclude any serious commitment to other creative endeavors. Undoubtedly, matters of opportunity and life setting play a very large role in the relative accomplishments of the two sexes. That this is not the whole story, however, is suggested by a study of Radcliffe Ph.D.'s, in which it was found that the women Ph.D.'s who had taken academic posts had published substantially less than their male counterparts, and that this was just as true of unmarried academic women as it was of married ones. . . . (119)

Some of the major sex differences we have noted—some appearing at a fairly early age—do not appear to have any direct relevance to adult sex roles, actual or anticipated. Does a girl of nine do poorly on an embedded-figures test because she thinks that this kind of skill is not going to be important for her later on in life, and well on a spelling test because she thinks this kind of skill is going to be important? It is doubtful whether either children or adults see those ability areas where we have detected the greatest sex differences as sex-role specific. This is not to say that sex-typing is irrelevant to intellectual development. But it is doubtful whether the sex differences in spatial ability, analytic style, and breaking set can be understood in terms of their greater direct relevance to the role requirements of one sex or the other.

Opportunities to Learn

Do the sexes differ in their opportunities to learn the skills and content of the ability areas where stable sex differences have been found? It has been widely assumed that girls' early verbal superiority might be due to their spending more time with adults, particularly with their mothers. From research on birth order and experimental studies of the effects of verbal interaction with adults in language acquisition, it may be safely inferred that the amount of a child's contact with adults does influence his language development. Preschool girls are kept at home with their mothers, the argument goes, while boys are allowed to go out to play with age-mates. . . . But when children enter school, and boys are exposed to intensive stimulation from the teacher, they catch up. A weakness of this argument is that it does not explain why boys catch up in vocabulary and reading comprehension, but not in fluency, spelling, and grammar. And furthermore, we lack direct evidence that preschool girls are kept at home more. Although it fits our stereotypes of the two sexes to think of girls as more protected, we must consider the possibility that girls may actually be given more freedom than boys. Because girls mature faster, perhaps parents can trust them sooner than boys to play away from home with little adult supervision. . . .

Similarly, it has been suggested that boys acquire greater spatial and perceptual-analytic ability because they have more opportunity to explore their environment at an early age—more opportunity to manipulate objects. Again, we have no evidence that this is so. It is true that if one watches nursery school children at play, one is more likely to find boys building with blocks and girls placing doll furniture in a doll house or pretending to cook with beaters and bowls; but it is difficult to see why one of these kinds of object manipulation should lead to greater spatial ability than the other. We know little about what kinds of learning experiences are involved when a child dissects stimuli (as the analytical, field-independent child does) instead of responding to them globally, but it is difficult to see why sheer quantity of stimulus exposure should make a difference beyond a certain point. . . .

"Identification" and Modeling

It has been thought that girls may be more verbal and boys more quantitative because children tend to model themselves primarily upon the same-sex parent. (20) Since mothers are typically more verbal and fathers typically more skilled at quantitative tasks, the argument goes, modeling the same-sex parent will produce differential patterns of abilities in boys and girls.

There are a number of difficulties with this explanation of the typical sex differences in ability profiles. Not all aspects of intellectual functioning are susceptible to modeling. Vocabulary and verbal fluency are aspects of a parent's intellectual equipment that a child can copy. Normally, his spelling is not. Yet girls maintain superiority throughout the school years in spelling and fluency, though not in vocabulary. Much of a parent's quantitative reasoning is done covertly, so that it is not accessible for copying, and very little spatial thinking is communicated from parent to child. Yet it is in spatial performance that we find the most consistent sex differences.

Sex differences in verbal ability occur at a very early age, long before the child is able to identify which parent is the same sex as himself, and long before he begins to copy same-sex models differentially. (86) Sex differences in verbal ability decline during the age period when the rise of identification and differential modeling ought to increase them. And consistent sex differences in quantitative ability do not appear until adolescence, long after the time when boys and girls have begun to prefer same-sex models. For these reasons we do not believe that the identification hypothesis provides an adequate explanation of the sex differences in ability profiles noted at the beginning of this chapter.

Sex-Typed
Personality Traits
as Mediating Processes

Numerous studies have shown that girls are more conforming, more suggestible, and more dependent upon the opinion of others than boys. And as mentioned earlier in this chapter, a number of studies have demonstrated that these very personality traits are associated with 1) field dependency (global perceiving), and 2) lack of ability to break set or restructure in problem solving. Witkin et al. have suggested that herein lies the explanation of sex differences in field independence and analytic style—that girls are more field-dependent and less analytical because of their greater conformity and eagerness to please. (163)

Why should there be any relationship between the cluster of personality dispositions that we may call the dependency cluster and individuals' characteristic modes of dealing with a stimulus array? Little is known about these relationships, and we can only speculate. First, an individual who is dependent and conforming is oriented toward stimuli emanating from other people; perhaps he finds it difficult to ignore these stimuli in favor of internal thought processes. Analytic thinking appears to require more internal "processing"; Kagan et al., have shown it to be associated with longer reaction times than global responding. (80) Dependent children have been shown to be more distractible; (120) their internal processing is interrupted, perhaps because of their greater orientation toward external interpersonal cues. This orientation probably helps them in certain kinds of intellectual performance; they should do better in recognizing names and faces, for example. But tasks calling for sequential thought may be hindered by a heavy reliance on external, interpersonal cues.

A second dimension of personality that might conceivably have a bearing upon the mode of dealing with a stimulus array in problem solving is the active-passive dimension. The passive person waits to be acted upon by the environment. The active person takes the initiative. Intellectual tasks differ in how much activity they require, so that the passive person is more at a disadvantage on some tasks than others. Vocabulary tests, for example, depend upon previously established associations, and therefore involve less trial and error than tasks that require restructuring or finding the answer to a previously unsolved problem.

We are suggesting, then, that either dependency or passivity may interfere with certain aspects of intellectual functioning. There are other aspects of intellectual performance that dependency may facilitate—achievement, for example. P. S. Sears has found that, among girls, projective measures of "need affiliation" are positively related to academic achievement. . . . (131)

On the basis of the above considerations, we find it plausible to believe that some of the sex differences outlined in the first section of the chapter may be traced to boys' greater independence and activity, girls' greater conformity and passivity. We do not know whether these personality differences between the sexes (if indeed they *are* consistent differences) are in any degree innate, or whether they are entirely a product of the social learning involved in the acquisition of sex roles; but we do suggest that the existence of the differences may have a bearing upon the intellectual development of the two sexes.

A second theory concerning the origins of sex differences in intellectual functioning may be derived from MacKinnon. We noted earlier that high I.Q., and more particularly creativity and originality, appear to be associated with cross-sex-typing in both sexes. MacKinnon has suggested that this may be due to the absence of repression. He argues that a man can only achieve a high degree of "masculinity" (as our culture defines it) by repressing the feminine character elements that all men possess. And presumably the converse would be true of women. . . . Repression, MacKinnon argues, has a generalized impact upon thought processes, interfering with the accessibility of the individual's own previous experiences. An individual who is using repression as a defense mechanism cannot be, to use MacKinnon's term, "fluent in scanning thoughts." MacKinnon has evidence that creativity is in fact associated with the absence of repression . . . and Barron reports that originality is associated with "responsiveness to impulse and emotion." Witkin reports that his field-independent people are less likely to use repression as a defense mechanism than his field-dependent people. If MacKinnon is right, this should mean that field-independent men are somewhat more feminine than field-dependent men. . . .

If MacKinnon's hypothesis is to be used to explain sex differences in intellectual performance, we would have to assume that women typically repress more than men, since they are more "field-dependent" and less adept at breaking set than men. It is difficult to see why a girl should have to repress her masculine tendencies more strongly than a boy does his feminine tendencies; on the contrary, social pressure is much stronger against a boy who is a sissy than against a girl who is a tomboy. Furthermore, women are freer to express feelings (with the exception of hostility) than men in our society. Hence it is difficult to characterize women as generally subject to repression. Furthermore, while it is true that they are more field-dependent, women are not any less "fluent in scanning thoughts," if we take their performance on divergent thinking and verbal-fluency tests as an indicator. Some aspects of women's intellectual performance, then, could be attributed to repression if there were evidence of greater repression in women, but others could not.

There appears to be some contradiction between the prediction that we could make on the basis of MacKinnon's repression theory and the prediction from Witkin's theory about dependency. To be creative, MacKinnon says, a man must be able to accept and express the feminine aspects of his character. Surely, one element of this femininity would be passive-dependency. Yet, passive-dependency, we have argued earlier, interferes with analytic thinking and some aspects of creativity. It would appear that the correlation between intellectual performance and cross-sex-typing ought to be stronger for women than for men, since among women masculinity implies both independence and absence of repression—two positive factors in intellectual performance. For men, however, femininity implies absence of repression (a positive factor) and passive-dependency (a negative factor). As we noted earlier, the evidence for cross-sex-typing as a correlate of intellectual abilities is stronger for women than for men.

So far, we have been discussing two mediating factors—repression and passive-dependency—which presumably affect both sexes in the same way. We noted earlier, however, that there were several traits, such as impulsiveness, aggression, and hyperkinesis, which appeared to be positive correlates for girls and negative ones for boys. . . .

How can a mediating process facilitate or inhibit intellectual growth for one sex and not the other? We do not think it necessary to suppose that different psychological principles govern the intellectual development of the two sexes; therefore we would like to explore two alternative possibilities to explain these opposite-direction effects. The first is that we have not been measuring comparable processes in the two sexes, and that when we specify the variables more exactly, same-direction correlations will emerge. For example, when we measure total activity level, we might get opposite correlations for the two sexes between activity level and measures of intellectual performance, because a high total activity level may have a different "meaning" for the two sexes, in the sense that it forms part of a different constellation of attributes. There is some indication from a study on activity level that this is the case. (93) But if we measure a selected aspect of activity, such as the ability to inhibit motor movement or the amount of intersituational variation in activity, we can and do obtain correlations with intellectual performance that are similar for both sexes. It is also possible that scores on total aggression will not relate clearly to intellectual performance, while scores that reflect whether the aggression is directed and instrumental would do so. If these distinctions were made in the measurement of aggression, the sex differences in the way aggression correlates with cognitive performance might well disappear.

The second possible explanation of these opposite-direction correlations involves an assumption of curvilinearity. Let us assume that there is a single personality dimension, running from passive and inhibited at one end of the scale to bold, impulsive, and hyperactive at the other. A tentative hypothesis might be that there is a curvilinear relationship between this dimension and intellectual performance, so that both the very inhibited and the very bold will perform less well, while those who occupy the intermediate positions on the inhibited-impulsiveness dimension will perform optimally. We suggest further that boys and girls, on the average, occupy different positions on the dimension we have described. There is reason to believe that boys are more aggressive, more active, and less passive than girls. Whether the differences are innate or the outcome of social learning is not so important here. The important point is that these temperamental differences do exist. The situation that we hypothesize may be graphed as follows:

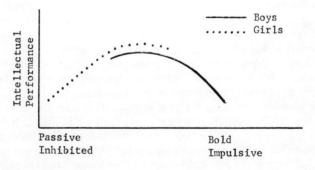

If the hypothesis holds, it would follow that for optimum intellectual performance, most girls need to become less passive and inhibited, while most boys need to become less impulsive. However, for those girls who do happen to be highly impulsive (as much so as the average boy, or even more so), impulsiveness should be a negative factor, as timidity should be for those boys at the passive end of the scale.

A parallel analysis may be made of anxiety as it affects intellectual performance in the two sexes. There is substantial evidence (beginning with the theoretical formulation of the problem by J. A. Taylor and K. W. Spence [147]) that the relation of anxiety to performance is curvilinear. Either very high or very low levels of anxiety interfere with performance on a variety of tasks; intermediate levels facilitate performance. If women and girls have a high base level of anxiety, then increases in anxiety above their base level will frequently carry them past the optimum point of the curve, and result in inhibition or disorganization of performance. If boys and men have a low base level of anxiety, increases in anxiety will more often either improve performance, or move them through the middle portions of the curve where changes in performance would not be found.

In evaluating this hypothesis, we must first ask whether the two sexes do in fact differ in their base level of anxiety. . . . There is very strong evidence for greater anxiety in girls when anxiety is measured with paper-and-pencil tests like the CMAS or TASC. However, the tendency for girls to score higher in anxiety on these tests has been attributed to their greater willingness to admit to such feelings, and is not conclusive evidence that any more basic difference exists. The answer to the question will no doubt depend upon how anxiety is defined. In two studies that measure physiological reactions to stress, females were found to have greater autonomic reactivity. (14; 139) A. T. Jersild and F. B. Holmes presented standardized fear situations in a laboratory situation to children of nursery school age, and obtained higher average "fear" scores for girls than boys. . . .(75)   With these various pieces of evidence in mind, we believe it to be a reasonable hypothesis that girls do have a higher base anxiety level than boys, so that increments from this base level might be expected to have a different effect for the two sexes.

We have so far discussed two "personality" dimensions that might bear a curvilinear relation to intellectual performance: anxiety, and a dimension running from inhibited-passive to bold-impulsive. Neither of these dimensions is precisely defined; if we wish to test the validity of the formulation, we must specify more exactly the behavioral dispositions that distinguish the sexes and bear the hypothesized curvilinear relation to intellectual performance. We must note, for example, that although the sexes do differ on such aspects of "impulsivity" as frequency of temper tantrums, aggression, and activity, they do not consistently differ on the "reflectivity-impulsivity" dimension,(81) so that this aspect of impulsivity would not be relevant to the explanation of sex differences offered here. Further differentiation will also be needed on the "intellectual performance" dimension. It is quite possible, for example, that "analytic style" and performance on spatial tests are related to impulsiveness or anxiety in the manner described, while certain aspects of verbal ability are not.

Genetic Versus Environmental Contributions

In the preceding section, we have discussed sex differences in personality traits as possible mediators of differences in intellectual performance. Assuming that the evidence is sufficient to convince the reader that there is indeed a substantial probability that such attributes as fearfulness, impulsiveness, independence, etc., do have a bearing on intellectual functioning, then it may be valuable to consider briefly the origins of the sex differences in these personality traits, with a view to discovering if the intellectual characteristics of either sex are likely to change as cultural conditions change. To what extent are boys more active or more aggressive because they are trained to adopt these socially defined sex-appropriate characteristics, and to what extent are they more active because of a substratum of biological determination with which environmental inputs must interact? W. Mischel has taken a social-learning point of view, arguing that the known socialization inputs to the two sexes are sufficiently different in the appropriate ways to produce known sex differences in dependency and aggression (and by implication in other personality traits as well).(108) D. A. Hamburg and D. T. Lunde, on the other hand, have presented evidence that in primates sex-specific hormones govern not only specifically sexual behavior, but also various kinds of social behavior. (62) Male-hormone treatment administered to a pregnant animal increases the incidence among the female offspring of rough-and-tumble play, and decreases the tendency to withdraw from the initiations, threats, and approaches of others. An interesting point emerging from Hamburg's report is that sex differences in social behavior may be related to endocrine influences even though there is no detectable sex difference in hormone concentrations at the time the behavior is observed. This point is important because of the fact that present methods of measurement do not reveal any differences between young boys and girls in the concentration of male or female hormones present in their bodies, even though their social behavior might suggest the presence of such a difference. This might be taken to mean that the differences in social behavior could not be a product of differential hormonal factors in the two sexes. Hamburg points to the possibility that hormonal "sensitization" during the prenatal period may contribute to the arousal of sex-appropriate behavior later in the life cycle, when the specific hormone concentrations are no longer present.

R. G. D'Andrade, analyzing the cross-cultural evidence, notes that certain temperamental differences seem to be cross-culturally universal, and are found even in societies where most of the usual environmental pressures toward sex-typing are absent (e.g., the Kibbutzim in Israel).(32) He also suggests that certain differential behavior in the two sexes is directly conditioned by such physical differences as size, strength, and biological role in the bearing and suckling of children; these differences are then generalized to similar activities and become institutionalized in occupational roles and other cultural prescriptions, in preparation for which anticipatory sex-typing occurs in childhood.

Let us assume, then, that the sex-typed attributes of personality and temperament which we have found to be related to intellectual functioning are the product of the interweaving of differential social demands with certain biological determinants that help to produce or augment differential cultural demands upon the two sexes. The biological underpinnings of the social demands for sex-typed behavior set modal tendencies for cultural demands, and set limits to the range of variation of these demands from one cultural setting to another. Still, within these limits considerable variation does occur, between families, between cultures, and in the nature of the behavior that a social group stereotypes as "feminine" or "masculine." Is there any evidence that such variations are associated with the nature or quality of intellectual performance in the two sexes?

In an attempt to measure cultural influences outside the home, P. Minuchin compared the performances of boys and girls in "modern" and "traditional" schools.(107) In this study, an effort was made to control for social class and intellectual ability of the children, in order to isolate the effects of the two school atmospheres. In the traditional school, behavior was more sex-typed during play sessions than in the modern school. And in intellectual tasks, there were greater sex differences in problem solving and coding tasks in the traditional schools than in the modern ones. These findings would be consistent with the hypothesis that strong social demands for sex-typed behavior, such as aggression in boys and conformity-passivity in girls, play a role in producing some of the sex differences we have seen in intellectual performance. The proof of this point, however, would rest on experimental attempts to change the nature of intellectual performance through changes in the social expectations for sex-typed behavior. . . . G. L. Carey attempted to improve problem-solving behavior by changing "attitudes" toward such behavior.(19) Group discussions directed toward improving the subjects' self-confidence in problem-solving tasks were held; these discussions emphasized the fact that it was socially acceptable to excel at problem solving. The discussion sessions improved the performance of college women but not of college men, suggesting that beliefs that skill in problem solving was not appropriate behavior had been an impediment to the normal performance of women but not of men. . . .

The findings on socialization practices within families, as they relate to intellectual development in the two sexes, point first of all to the fact that the environmental factors embodied in parent-child interaction do indeed make a difference in the child's intellectual performance. But more importantly, these findings indicate that the same environmental input affects the two sexes differently, and that different factors are associated with optimal performance for boys and girls. The brighter girls tend to be the ones who have not been tied closely to their mother's apron strings, but have been allowed and encouraged to fend for themselves. The brighter boys, on the other hand, have had high maternal warmth and protection in early childhood. We find, then, that environmental effects are not merely something added to, or superimposed upon, whatever innate temperamental differences there are that affect intellectual functioning. Rather, there is a complex interaction. The two sexes would appear to have somewhat different intellectual strengths and weaknesses, and hence different influences serve to counteract the weaknesses and augment the strengths.

Part Two

Schools and Preschools

I know that the elevation of the female mind, by means of moral, physical, and religious truth, is considered by some men as unfriendly to the domestic character of a woman. But this is a prejudice of little minds and springs from the same spirit which opposes the general diffusion of knowledge among the citizens of our republic.

B. Rush
"Thoughts upon Female
Education, . . ."
1787

III

He Only Does It To Annoy . . .

Marshall P. Smith

In the Head Start room there were ten children. Four were boys. Girls were playing busily at a variety of games—jigsaw puzzles, toy sink, stove, coloring books, costumes. The four boys were building and knocking down a tower of blocks in the corner.

Two weeks later I came back. Some girls were playing busily at a variety of games. Three boys were building and knocking down a tower of blocks in the corner. Two girls were fussing over the fourth boy who was wearing a 1920-style lady's hat. The teacher was amused.

Two weeks still later, two of the building boys were building separate towers and approaching a fight over the division of available blocks. The other two boys, the teacher's arm around one of them, were sitting on the floor closely attending the group vocabulary lesson on household utensils. I was not amused.

Up to at least fourteen years of age, from preschool on, boys and girls are generally in mixed boy-girl classes and are taught by women teachers. There is prevalent lore to the effect that boys suffer from this, that they are "feminized," that they reject school work as "sissy." It seems clear that some do suffer, but it also seems clear that some profit.

Because boys make more waves in society, much of the concern about schools is about their effect on boys. Nevertheless, the evidence on girls, even though often presented incidentally or for comparison with boys, comes through with a modest suggestion. It might be that, while our school system generally hurts the intellectual development of some boys, it hurts that of girls even more.

Differences Start at or before Birth

Boys find early life hazardous. F. Bentzen points out that more boys than girls are stillborn.(13) Infant girls are healthier than infant boys. In the first year of life, P. Sexton finds more boys die of injury at birth, or of congenital malformations, or of circulatory diseases, or of diarrhea, or of influenza, or of pneumonia.(133) More boys die in accidents, more have disabling injuries, more are brain injured—the list goes on and on. Girls apparently start as better organisms.

Girls develop faster than boys. J. M. Tanner shows that girls at birth are about four weeks ahead of boys in skeletal age—an index of maturation—and maintain about 25 percent advantage in this regard until maturity. (146)

Girls and boys not only develop differently, they are treated differently by their parents—the differences in behavior and treatment appearing as early as three weeks of age.

Moss studied thirty children and their mothers in their homes doing "normal" things.(110) Sex differences in behavior were dramatic. Boys "fussed" significantly more at both three weeks and three months. They were much more irritable. At three weeks they spent more time awake and lying on their backs. Girls at both three weeks and three months spent much more time asleep. Mothers at three weeks gave significantly more attention to their little boys—attending them more, holding them, making them stand, and arousing them. Moss controlled for sleeping and still found that mothers tended to stimulate and arouse the boys more. But now with sleep controlled for, it was found the mothers did a great deal more imitating (cooing, talking, making faces) of the little girls than they did of the little boys. When irritability was controlled for, the boys still were more stimulated and aroused, the girls still were more imitated. It seems the mothers systematically encouraged general activity in their little boys even though the boys were already more irritable, a behavior which, if it persisted, would annoy a teacher. The mothers encouraged verbal behavior and social interaction in their little girls—both of these would give little girls a head start in nursery school and kindergarten.

Kagan and M. Lewis studied six-month-old infants on a variety of measures of attention and in a variety of sense modalities. They retested the same infants at thirteen months. They found, "The data are persuasive in suggesting that girls display more sustained attention to visual stimulation, and prefer more novel auditory patterns than boys at both six and thirteen months of age." (78) If these characteristics—sustained attention and preference for novelty—are measures of maturity, the girls are starting early to develop traits appropriate to school. On the other hand, little boys show characteristics during the preschool years which will not stand them well in school.

Little girls and boys begin to show distinctly different patterns of play behavior as early as thirteen months of age. These differences are of the sort found to differentiate "masculine" and "feminine" characteristics later in life. S. Goldberg and Lewis studied thirteen-month-old boys and girls in free play in the presence of their mothers. (54) Measures were obtained, for example, on reluctance to leave mother, on time spent vocalizing to mother, on time spent looking at mother, on time in area closest to mother, and on response to frustration. On all of the following comparisons, the boys differed significantly from the girls: girls spent more time touching their mothers and staying in close proximity; boys cried less at frustration and spent more time trying to solve the frustrating problems. Girls in frustration gestured more for help. Boys chose toys that required more gross motor activity, banging and swinging around. Boys were more active and vigorous. In other words, boys displayed many precursors of teacher disturbing behavior.

Girls have been shown to be emotionally more dependent on adults than boys are. B. McCandless, C. Bilous, and H. Bennett found that preschool girls tended more than boys to seek help from the teacher when they got into difficulties with other children. (99) Boys tended to be independent or aggressive in the same situation. Girls tended more than boys to move away from conflict and to give up what they were doing prior to the conflict.

Girls' behavior at this preschool age is just that which will offer gratification to the female teacher, helping her to feel nurturant and wanted, but at the same time, if it is reinforced, this dependent behavior may generate future problems in the girls' intellectual development. The boys, on the other hand, are showing behavior potentially conducive to intellectual growth.

Mischel shows that, by three years, boys are more aggressive physically, more negativistic, and noisier than girls. (109) They initiate more fights and fight back more, and these tendencies persist into the school years. And girls in general talk earlier and more than boys. D. McCarthy thoroughly reviews the literature and concludes: "The vast accumulation of evidence . . . certainly is convincing proof that a real sex difference in language development exists in favor of the girls." (100)

The Girls Are
Ready for the School

Not only do these more mature, talky little girls surpass boys in their development, they also are superior very early in some aspects of adjustment necessary for the first school adventure. The little girls are altogether readier for school. Maccoby and C. N. Jacklin note some critical points:

Girls are responsive to social cues earlier than boys, and react more positively to adults and strangers.

Girls are no less active than boys, but boys tend when they do act to put out more energy and respond with more movement.

Boys are more aggressive, more ready to attack or retaliate in interpersonal situations, but this aggressiveness does not generalize to problem solving situations. (95)

To the unsophisticated and slightly harassed preschool teacher, the socially responsive girls are a joy; the aggressive overacting boys are often less than enchanting.

So here we have ready for nursery school and kindergarten a giggle of girls who, as compared to little boys, are physiologically more mature, are more developed in language skills, have better attention spans, are more socially responsive, and are already being socialized by their mothers to meet the expectations of their teachers. We have a banging of boys: noisy, obstreperous, independent, not seeking help, starting fights—in a word, immature—and not very reinforcing to the teacher.

Three-year-old boys and girls show pronounced differences in their play. Teachers react differentially to these differences. B. I. Fagot and G. R. Patterson developed checklists of nursery school play and games to determine which were most popular with boys and which with girls. (43) Their listings were consistent for two different nursery schools and two different terms: boys built blocks, used transportation toys, climbed, rode tricycles, played in the sandbox. Girls painted, used kitchen toys, did artwork, played with dolls and the dollhouse, molded clay. These games were designated "sex appropriate," one set for boys (masculine), one for girls (feminine).

The four women teachers in the nursery classes were observed reacting to the children's play. Counting all teacher reinforcements, including those of neutral play, boys and girls received about equal attention. But of the number of times teachers reinforced boys for sex-appropriate play, 85 percent were for feminine behaviors. Of the times teachers reinforced girls for the critical behaviors, 97 percent were for feminine play. Among the children, boys reinforced boys and girls reinforced girls. In this same-sexed child mutual reinforcement, more than 99 percent of the time it was for sex-appropriate play. Thus girls supported "feminine" behavior in girls, and boys supported "masculine" behavior in boys, while the teachers supported "feminine" behavior for both. Despite the social pressure by the teachers the boys did not, over the year, adopt "feminine" play. Perhaps home reinforcement and that of their peers helped them hold to the "masculine" preferences and resist.

One measure of a child's identification with an adult figure is the amount of imitation of the model. Girls, being girls, should in early grades show more behavior imitative of their female teachers than do boys. P. Friedman and N. Bowers studied this question using as the critical factor student imitation of the verbal style of the female teacher. They used only teachers selected by observation as being "rewarding." Preschool, kindergarten, and first grade were studied. In terms of overall differences, girls showed significantly greater amounts of imitation than boys on four out of five measures. There was also a significant grade effect: "First grade students showed significantly more imitative behavior than either preschool or kindergarten [pupils]." (49) Girls showed a significant increase by imitation of emotionally toned (supportive/nonsupportive) speech. Boys showed no such increase, indicating no increase in behavior identifying with their teachers and therefore, perhaps, some divergence from the values of the school.

If girls should feel school-related activities are sex-appropriate for them, they should be motivated to do school work. Similarly, if boys are ambivalent about how they perceive school-related affairs in terms of sex appropriateness, their motivation and achievement should suffer. Kagan studied second and third grade boys and girls to discover how they sex-typed various school objects. He summarizes, "more young girls than boys view school activities as congruent with their sex role, and, consequently, they should be more highly motivated to master academic tasks." (76)

The School Is the Way the Children See It

To this point we have the primary school (preschool through third grade) situation. Girls' behavior seems to be favored by female teachers right from the start. Boys and girls both perceive the school as a feminine environment. Boys, far more than girls, resist the school values—quiet, control of aggression, orderliness, and attention. This boy-girl difference in attitude and perception should influence performance, and it seems to.

Beginning reading usually calls for a sharp reduction in freedom of pupil interaction, a necessary condition for peer reinforcement, and a corresponding increase in teacher demand for attention and structure. A teacher, to survive, must reinforce docility, conformity, and impulse control. These behaviors are not only necessary in the standard teaching situation but also are congruent with so-called feminine behavior. The teacher finds these agreeable behaviors being demonstrated by girls and their disagreeable opposites by boys. Her personal values match those she needs to run her class. It is reasonable to suppose that she will positively reinforce girls and also boys who behave like girls. She may, if only by omission of approval, show disapproval of boys who behave in a "masculine" way. It is also reasonable to suppose that girls, reinforced for "nice" behavior, may come to see this approval as the main psychic increment to be gained from the school.

J. D. McNeil investigated the problem of the relation between teacher disapproval and reading difficulties.(102) In a two-part study he first had two groups of kindergarten children, 72 boys and 60 girls, "equal" in reading readiness, work through a teaching machine program which taught 40 new words in daily lessons over three weeks. During the programmed lesson each child made individual responses and received individual feedback. Each child, in his separate cubicle, was presented the material at a common pace. Encouraging comments, identical, were received by each child from a tape. The same number of responses were demanded of all children. In this programmed instruction phase, the boys earned scores significantly higher than those of the girls.

In the second phase, the following year, seven female first grade teachers taught the 93 children remaining from the original group. Standard reading materials and methods were used: direct instruction, reading groups, and seat work. After four months the children were tested on a sample of the words taught by the teachers. The girls scored significantly higher than the boys.

McNeil found that the first grade teachers were perceived by the children as discriminating against the boys. Boys were seen as receiving significantly more negative admonitions than girls. Boys were seen as being given significantly less opportunity to read than were girls. Teachers assessed boys as having little motivation or readiness for reading significantly more often than they did girls. And McNeil found that for individual boys the drop in standing from the first part of the study to the second was significantly correlated both with the perceived number of negative teacher comments and with perceived deprivation of opportunity to read.

McNeil used student reports to find the children's perception of teacher favoritism toward girls in first grade reading. That was how the children, both boys and girls, saw it. But O. Davis and J. Slobodian in an observational study found the children were wrong.(36) They found that teachers were quite impartial in awarding chances for reading and that they criticized boys no more than they did girls. But they found also that McNeil was right. Their children, in interview, also perceived the teachers as criticizing boys more and the girls as reading better than the boys. So the teachers did it one way and the children saw it another. It is noteworthy that, although the teachers were impartial in their overt behavior toward the children, they nevertheless rated significantly more boys as "less motivated and ready" than girls.

T. L. Good and J. E. Brophy asked why this mistaken perception by the children should occur.(56) They observed a reading situation and found no sex-related favoritism in criticism, support, opportunities to read, or reading problems, though in the reading class teachers did significantly favor the high achievement students by hinting or rephrasing questions. The reason for the children's misperceptions was suggested by observations of their general classroom activities. In the general situation the more disruptive behavior of the boys resulted in their being the target of significantly more criticism than the girls, even though the boys offered more correct answers. In particular the boys with low achievement were criticized in 33 percent of their one-to-one contacts with the teacher; low achievement girls were criticized 16 percent of the time. Correspondingly and consistently the high achievement boys and girls were criticized 13 and 8 percent of the time, respectively.

It would be nice to have firm evidence of teacher fairness, but the payoff anyway is how the child sees it. If he/she sees the teacher as picking on him/her, she (the teacher) and what she is associated with will become aversive. If the little girl sees herself as relatively favored, the school situation becomes positive. For the little boy it becomes negative.

The discrepancy between the observed teacher behavior and the child's perception of it may be, in part, due to a problem inherent in short-term observation by an outsider. An outside observer does not have time to learn the unconscious turns of phrase and tones of voice the teacher uses in communication with children. Children in a classroom, highly attuned to the attitudes of important adults, have had plenty of time to learn the signs. It may be that an objective observational tally of a teacher's verbal communications to a child misses what the child really hears and sees—the slightly tenser, higher tone, the pause with the chin up, the patient sigh. Children are mightily perceptive, as any parent knows. Children actually do respond to the expectations of their teachers. No amount of controversy that has attended the R. Rosenthal and L. Jacobson results (124)—see also Rosenthal and Rubin (125)—dissuades us from the intuitive recognition that subtle signals from teachers are desperately important to children.

N. J. Anastasiow factor-analyzed teacher ratings on boys' characteristics in early school. (3) Kindergarten teachers used just one global factor, readiness. First grade teachers distinguished two. One of these, "school competence," included high loadings on success in first grade, social virtues, readiness, constructive play, and maturity. The second factor, "physical competence," had high loadings on masculinity, physical ability, and outdoor versus indoor play. This change from preschool to first grade in teacher interpretation of boys' behavior is perhaps the start of the pattern of teacher discrimination against boys. Kindergarten teachers see just readiness. First grade teachers distinguish between school readiness and masculinity. We are not amused.

Upper Grades—More of the Same

Women teachers, at least in upper grades, do indeed subject boys to more disapproval than they do girls, and the boys and girls know it. By the sixth grade the message is loud and clear. W. J. Meyer and G. G. Thompson made an observational study of three classrooms over an extended term.(104)   Boys significantly more often than girls were the target of disapproving contacts from the teacher—the differences for three different classrooms were on the average about five times more disapproval for boys than girls. The experimenters asked also for students' feelings about who got disapproval and who got praise. Here, again, both boys and girls see boys as getting significantly more punishing contacts. And the tendency, though it is not significant, is for the children to see the girls getting more approval. Meyer and Thompson feel that these patterns of real and child-perceived disapproval of boys by female teachers reflect the code of the school. Aggressive boys, noisy and full of energy, upset the even order of the class. The teacher tries to put this down by admonition and punishment. The boys and girls know this.

Whether the teachers like it or not, children in the grades see boys as criticized by teachers more often than girls, and how the child sees it is the thing that matters. The question is, does criticism hurt performance? The answer is, it does. S. A. Allen, P. S. Spear, and J. R. Lucke studied the reactions in complex learning situations of primary level (first and second grade) and intermediate level (fifth and sixth grade) boys and girls under conditions of approval, silence, and criticism. They were interested in the children's motivation, learning, and retention. On the measures of motivation the younger boys were significantly more adversely affected by criticism than any other group. In general, the children made more errors under criticism than under praise or silence, and a significantly fewer number stayed with the task and reached criterion performance. Twice as many "praise" and "silence" children reached criterion performance. Criticized young children spent significantly more time at the retention task and in general had a tendency to make more errors. Allen, Spear, and Lucke found: "criticism interferes most strongly with younger boys' performance, followed by the performances of older girls, younger girls, and older boys, in that order." (1)

It is noteworthy that the older boys are least affected by criticism—perhaps they have become inured to what they perceive is a way of life; at the same time the performances of older girls are affected more adversely than those of younger girls—perhaps they have identified more with the women experimenters and their teachers or perhaps they are more motivated to achieve in school and, therefore, more vulnerable.

There is a clear interrelation between perceived teacher approval and the payoff—children's academic achievement. H. H. Davidson and G. Lang studied children in the upper half of their classes in reading ability in the fourth, fifth, and sixth grades. (33) The children who thought the teacher approved of them performed significantly better than those who felt less approved. Those children who perceived teacher approval, also, according to teacher judgment, behaved better than those who saw teacher disapproval. This works out to a kind of four-way parlay. Children who approved themselves perceived the teacher as approving them, behaved better, and achieved better. Boys as usual got the short end. Girls thought teachers liked them; boys were more negative. Teachers (nine women, one man) rated girls as better students—though not significantly.

Davidson and Lang considered socioeconomic status (SES). Would anyone be surprised that low SES children had a poorer perception of themselves and achieved less or that teachers found their behavior more undesirable? It comes down to the proposition that if you want a child to have a hard time in school, make him an elementary schoolboy of low SES. And if he is black, so much the worse.

In Evanston, J. Hsia carried through a study of integration from 1967 to 1971.(69)   Teachers rated first and second grade children on a number of behavioral characteristics. The list reveals the values of the school:

Plays well with others
Respects rights and property of others
Is developing self-discipline
Accepts responsibility
Is courteous
Follows directions
Works well alone
Works well with others
Completes assignments in reasonable time
Works carefully and neatly
Uses time and materials well
Shows initiative

This is a nice list of nice values. Any elementary teacher, or junior or senior high teacher for that matter, could write it in her sleep.

On the Evanston list of good behavior, teachers rated first graders from good to less good in the consistent order: white girls, white boys, black girls, black boys. For the same children the following year the order was the same, and within each year the differences between groups were significant. The investigators sought any meliorating effects of desegregation between the first and second year; they found none.

Almost the same ranking, in reverse, was found for referrals to school psychologists, social workers, and counselors. Here the problem boy pattern recurred: black boys most, white boys next, black girls next, and white girls the least. Teacher comments in the cumulative records showed the same general trend. For grades 2, 4, and 5 after desegregation, the percentages of children receiving negative teacher comments were black boys 25 percent, black girls 17 percent, white boys 15 percent, and white girls 5 percent.

The irony in the situation is that objective recording of pupil behavior for grades 1 and 2 yielded ". . . no differences between black and white pupils' behavior in most categories. The nature of adult-pupil interactions, the quality of peer group interactions, use of materials, physical space and equipment, signs of emotion, and group size all failed to distinguish behavior of black pupils from whites." (69) Thus, selective teacher perception in this study puts the black boys down as it puts boys down in general.

Girls Get the A's But the Boys Grow

Just as the children see the teacher as less favorable toward boys, boys are seen by teachers as having attitudes toward school less favorable than those of girls. The corollaries are obvious—teachers will expect lower academic performance from boys, and boys will expect to get lower grades. Lower grades are what they get. Maccoby says: "Girls get better grades than boys throughout the school years, even in subjects in which boys score higher on standard achievement tests." (92)

But girls usually score higher on reading tests. A. Gates did a national study of differences in reading in the public schools at various grade levels. He tested on speed, vocabulary, and comprehension. In grades two through eight the mean raw score for girls was higher on every comparison than that of boys. Of 21 comparisons, girls were significantly superior on 17. It is noteworthy that the lower mean scores for boys were depressed by the "large proportion of boys [who] obtained the lowest scores without a corresponding increase in the number obtaining top scores." Gates suggests that

more girls than boys pursue a kind of life in which more respect, more incentives, and more opportunities for reading appear earlier and persist longer. Contrariwise, more boys than girls may find little or no early need for learning. These boys fall behind girls at the beginning, and a relatively large number of them remain in the conspiciously poor reading group throughout the grades.

Boys as a group seem to get the worst of the school situation on a whole variety of indicators. In a study of the ninth grade classes in a semisuburban area, Sexton intensively studied approximately 1,000 students.(133)   She found:

- 77 percent of school referrals to psychiatric help were boys
- 79 percent of students in corrective mental institutions were boys
- 72 percent of serious problem cases (law breakers and truants) were boys
- 65 percent of misbehavior referrals to school counselors were boys
- 66 percent of those in "remedial mentally retarded" classes were boys

When Sexton examined scholastic performance of tenth and twelfth grade students in the same school system she found:

- 11 percent of boys were failures in all their studies—about twice the rate for girls
- 37 percent of boys and 25 percent of girls had D or F averages in the tenth grade—in twelfth grade it was 26 percent of boys and 6 percent of girls
- Of honor students only 38 percent were boys

Other studies have found the same sort of evidence that boys get less than a fair shake in grading practices in schools. R. S. Carter investigated grading in beginning algebra classes of which three were taught by women and three by men. The teachers were well matched in certification, experience, and training. He established four groupings: boys taught by men, girls taught by men, boys taught by women, girls taught by women. At the end of the study he found no significant differences in mental ability among groups. There were no significant differences in algebra achievement either among his groups or by totals: girls versus boys, or women teachers versus men teachers. There were no measurable ability or achievement differences involved. But differences in algebra grades as posted in the students' records were dramatic:

- Women teachers gave significantly higher grades than men
- Girls were awarded significantly higher grades than boys
- Girls' marks were significantly higher than boys' regardless of the sex of the teacher

Carter concludes, "The data used in this investigation proved that there is a slight overrating of girls generally and an underrating of boys, especially by women teachers." (22)

This business of boys getting a bad break in schools does not happen only in this country. M. Wisenthal studied census reports of the United States, Canada, and New Zealand, analyzing age-grade tables. He found: ". . . highly significant differences in favor of boys in the number of children shown as overage for all school grades above three (9-year-olds) . . . highly significant differences in favor of girls in the numbers shown for underage and at-age in the same grades."(161)   Since the principal reason for falling back is failure, it is a virtual certainty that boys fail significantly more than girls.

It is clear that boys and girls get differential treatment through the grades with the boys apparently getting the worst of it. But with all this, the girls as a group seem to suffer more than boys from their school experience. Not in grades, for there the girls excel, but they suffer in something more subtle. V. C. Crandall studied boys' and girls' levels of aspiration over the whole span of schooling.(28) Girls underestimated their ability consistently; boys overestimated their ability. Compared to their past performance, boys are overoptimistic, girls are pessimistic. Girls estimate their expected performance at new tasks lower than would be predicted from past performance. Boys' estimates are higher.

Perhaps this pattern of self-deprecation by the girls is also a function of the feminization of the class. Reinforced for nice behavior by higher grades, they come to depend on these symbols for the approval they need. S. R. Tulkin, J. P. Muller, and L. K. Conn found that girls with a high need for approval, as measured by a social desirability scale, were the most popular while boys with a high need for approval were least popular.(152)   As girls grow older and find teacher approval is not enough, they may sense that high academic ambition sets them apart and renders them less attractive to their peers. The original pattern of identification with the female teacher, and the increment of approval derived from her, may lead to more and more need for approval from peers and hence to lowered academic ambition. For the boys, the opposite trend may operate. Getting less approval from the teacher and needing less from their peers, they become, if they are not real dropouts, more self-motivated and more confident. Positive reinforcement then accrues to the boys for "masculine" independence behavior, for autonomy.

There is fairly consistent evidence, cited by Maccoby [See Chapter II in this book.], that important aspects of intellectual functioning, including high general intelligence, are associated with cross-sex typing; that is, "feminine" tending boys and "masculine" tending girls score higher than those of the same sex with "appropriate" sex orientation. Anastasiow found, however, a curvilinear relation between first grade reading and sex-role identification. (3) He identified "masculine" boys, "feminine" boys, and "sex-role confused" boys by their choice of sex-appropriate toys. The masculine boys scored significantly higher on reading than the sex-role confused boys but not significantly higher than the feminine boys. Boys having a hard time finding out who they were, had a hard time with reading.

It could be that here is a key to something. Note that the high "masculine" boys, who often act counter to the classroom norms, nevertheless achieve. Perhaps they are learning, and early, to make it on their own, resisting the socializing effects of the teacher but accepting the tasks of learning. And the "feminine" boys, who have modeled on the teacher, are accepting the school work and the teacher's reinforcements without conflict. Perhaps the confused boys will be the "trouble makers" and the "dropouts."

It is known girls get better grades than boys. It is known girls are better liked by their teachers than boys, and yet even the best of them fail the test of full intellectual development as compared with the best of the boys. Certainly the weaker girls seem to succeed more than the weaker boys in terms of dropping out, but what happens to the good ones? A cogent argument that girls are conditioned to be underachievers in school from the word go is presented by Women on

Words and Images, of Princeton, New Jersey. (165) They investigated the sex-related stereotypes in 134 elementary school readers. The report is devastating. Citing only a few of the dominant themes, they found for "active mastery" themes such as ingenuity, cleverness, industry, bravery, creative helpfulness, competence—boys cited 1,004 times, girls cited 342. For "second sex" themes such as passivity, pseudo-dependence, altruism, goal constriction, incompetence, humiliation of the opposite sex—boys cited 182 times, girls cited 435 times. It must take a pretty tough girl to resist the constant pressure to measure down to the girls of the stories.

Consider some correlates of high intellectual function as reported by Maccoby [See Chapter II in this book.]:

Impulse control . . . impulsiveness is a negative factor for at least some aspects of intellectual development in boys, but for girls it is a less negative—and perhaps even a positive—factor.

Impulse control is highly valued by teachers and is generally considered a "feminine" characteristic. Boys as boys seem to need more control; girls seem to need less if intellectual function is the criterion.

Fearfulness and anxiety Correlations between measures of anxiety and measures of aptitude or achievement are substantially negative for girls and women, while the correlations are either low negative, zero, or positive for boys and men.

Fearfulness and anxiety are generally considered to be more feminine than masculine and are not too severely frowned upon by elementary teachers. It seems again that boys to succeed should maybe have a little more of the characteristics, girls less.

Aggression and competitiveness . . . aggressiveness appears to be more of an inhibitor, or less of a facilitator, for intellectual development among boys than among girls . . . competitiveness was found to correlate with I.Q., and with progressive increases in I.Q., for both sexes, but the correlations are higher for girls than boys.

Aggressiveness and competitiveness are usually considered masculine and are not favored in the elementary school culture. Once again it seems girls need more and boys need less.

Level of aspiration and achievement motivation . . . the bulk of the findings seem to indicate that boys are more likely to rise to an intellectual challenge, girls to retreat from one.

Once more, girls to succeed should show more of this "masculine" characteristic.

Dependency, passivity, and independence For both sexes, there is a tendency for the more passive-dependent children to perform poorly on a variety of intellectual tasks, and for independent children to excel.

Passive dependency seems to be a positive value in the school culture; independence is often frowned upon by the teacher. Passive dependency is usually thought of, though perhaps wrongly, as feminine, independence as masculine. Girls to succeed should once again show more of the so-called masculine characteristics.

There is an abundance of evidence that boys (and men) surpass girls (and women) in many of the intellectual exercises that contribute to adult success:

- Witkin points out that boys and men tend to be more field independent than girls and women. (162)
- Kagan cites research showing boys are superior to girls in tasks involving reasoning and analysis. "Boys appear to be more analytic, more independent, and more persistent in problem solving in a laboratory situation. This difference increases with time . . ." (77)
- Maccoby reports a study showing unmarried women Ph.D.'s in academic posts had published much less than men. (92)
- Maccoby cites studies indicating that the brighter the girl the more expectations of her performance fall behind her ability, and that girls fear school failure more than boys and are more upset by it. (92)
- Kagan points to several studies showing that there is strong male involvement in mastery of academic subjects by the time of adolescence, while girls, who typically out-perform boys in the early grades, tend to fall back by adolescence. (77)

What has happened to the girls along the way? I think it is arguable that the schools are at fault. Coming eagerly into school, the little girl finds an approving teacher who puts great emphasis on being nice—in fact reinforces little girls for the behaviors of compliance, social responsiveness, dependency, and impulse control. The little girl sensitively sees the little boys admonished for behaviors of aggressiveness, independence, impulsiveness, and autonomy. She generalizes the approval she receives from the teacher to the habits of "niceness" and comes to see school subjects only as an adjunct, a vehicle for earning approval. At the same time the boy, that is if he lasts, has found approval elsewhere, in task mastery and in discovering his competencies. For him the teacher's approval gradually becomes incidental and his intellectual development is fostered.

On balance it seems the girls who resist the behavioral standards of the school, who are not "nicey nice," will profit thereby in intellectual function. It seems the boys who learn to control their impulses but refuse to become thoroughly socialized to the "feminine" school will profit. I suggest that our schools, in their impact on intellectual functioning, tend to constrict the variance of the girls and to increase the variance of the boys. The weak girls stay with it and conform. The strong girls surrender and become nice. The weak boys fail—often wanting to. The strong boys resist and make it.

What Way Out?

Maybe, just maybe, all-boy and all-girl classes might help. There is little hard evidence, but there are some hints.

The Fairfax County, Virginia, School Board in the early 1960's sponsored experiments with all-boy and all-girl classes in the third, fifth, and sixth grades. No special curricular changes were made in the way of "masculine" or "feminine" materials, nor were special teachers assigned. Nevertheless, J. F. Hurley reports that in achievement the one-sex classes consistently tended to do better than matched controls. (71; 72) One group was studied that had same-sexed classes in both the fifth and sixth grades. The boys in the second year group continued their considerable advantage over the controls. The girls did not. Hurley points out that boys were more eager for the second year than the girls. Perhaps this was because the girls at 11-12 years of age were rapidly approaching puberty while the boys were still well away.

In the fifth grade one-sex classes, boys were noisier, more enthusiastic, more experimental, and more imaginative than girls—a result to be expected if the early grades had done well their job of making the girls "nice." Boys seemed to be less inhibited than boys in mixed classes in displaying girl-type interests. Similarly girls seemed more ready to express interest in boy-type subjects and activities. Girls became somewhat less worried about grades and less concerned about covering up deficiencies than did girls in mixed classes. Hurley suggests that it was the boys of lower aptitude that benefited most from all-boy classes. It is just these boys that become, in regular classes, the behavior problems and the dropouts.

The data on which these behaviors are based are not firm enough to be quantified, but they do suggest a need for examining the possibilities of same-sex classes, not only to promote academic achievement, but also to free our children of stereotypes.

R. W. Strickler in a preliminary report cites enthusiastic support among teachers, parents, and children for one-sex classes. His early data indicate considerable reading gains by boys in all-boy classes compared with boys in mixed classes. (144)

Some of Strickler's informal observations are intriguing:

Several girls in the all-girl class assumed the more aggressive role usually played by boys.

Girls became more critical of mistakes made by other girls.

Girls became more active and had less regard for the "good girl" role which they usually play in a mixed group.

The usual "prime-year" work was quickly exhausted by the all-girl group.

Boys suffered fewer kindergarten adjustment problems when separated from girls.

A masculinized program was appropriate for girls, too. Girls related well to male resource persons and helpers, and enjoyed boy-oriented stories as well.

Boys developed more realistic self-concepts and more positive attitudes towards school when they were separated from girls.

It is hard to see these children as hurting. Strickler's program was designed specifically to "masculinize" the boys' school experience in order to foster their learning and improve their perception of the school. Things seem to be happening to the girls, too. Maybe Strickler, in searching for the boys, has discovered the girls.

IV

"Look, Jane, Look!
See Dick Run and Jump!
Admire Him!"

Karen DeCrow

In case the image of women has not been totally instilled in a little girl before she is five years old, by television and by her parents and friends, school finishes the job. Teachers are individuals, and school curricula vary from locale to locale, so it can be argued that there is no uniform content. However, one crucial item in the educative process is standard: the textbook.

Every month several small textbook companies are bought by the few giants. There are about fifteen major textbook companies which control about 90 percent of the textbook market. They watch each other closely and produce very similar products. And they have the image of woman as helpmate, as mother, as *observer* of male activities, included in every book. School attendance is compulsory in this country. This means that every young girl *must* read about herself as passive citizen for twelve years—by law.

Textbook Content and Women

As a former textbook editor I was aware of this image, but I did not know how prevalent it was until I studied textbooks, grades Kindergarten through 3.(37) I did a content analysis of social studies books and readers put out by ten companies. In this group of textbooks, no women worked outside the home except as a teacher or a nurse. The teachers and nurses were Miss, indicating clearly that when a woman marries she leaves her profession. This in spite of the fact that over half the women in the United States are employed outside the home; one-third of the women with preschool children work; and 40 percent of the mothers of school-age children are employed.

No man was shown as doing anything except going to work outside the home, as a full-time occupation. None were students, none were unemployed, none did housework, except "men's work" such as gardening and taking out the garbage.

The *decision-making* for the family was done by men. This included decisions about household matters. For example, in one story, the children want to build a sandbox. They are told by the mother (the full-time mother) to wait and ask Father how to do it when he gets home.

Girls do most of the work helping Mother: washing the dishes, caring for the baby, setting the table, etc. Boys also help Mother, but Father does not. The clear implication is that when the boy grows up he will be a father, and not do the work of women and children. In one story the family has a new baby and everyone is chipping in to "help Mother" with "her" work. Father is carrying the laundry, but the poor man cannot manage it. He stumbles and trips and laundry spills out of the basket. The children say "Poor Father." Here we are supposed to believe that an adult male, who presumably earns enough money to support a family of five, does not have what it takes to get the laundry done. The lesson is clearly that Father may help out in an emergency, but his job is not keeping the clothes clean.

The youngest child (usually female) is always saved from danger by the oldest child (always male). Father provides all the good times for the family, and also solves the problems. In one story, the family is going on a car trip (100 miles) to visit Grandmother and Grandfather. Mother says wait until Father comes home. He will read his map (the implication is that she doesn't do that big intellectual stuff), and plan how to make the trip (100 miles down the superhighway). The family is pictured sitting around Father, watching him plan the trip. In textbook illustrations, whenever the whole family is in the car, *Father always is driving,* with Mother sitting by his side.

Despite the fact that many mothers work outside the home, the mothers in the textbooks (ideals) are at home. One story shows a little boy coming home from school. (70) "Where is Mother?" The implication is that at three o'clock in the afternoon every woman has to be at home. The child shows signs of anxiety when he does not see his mother around. He goes into the kitchen and sees the pots steaming. He says that he knows Mother is at home. We know what Mother does at home. She doesn't make pottery, or snooze on the couch. She cooks, at three o'clock in the afternoon. In addition to the idea that Mother must be home at all times, is the suggestion that children are not encouraged to be autonomous. These stories take place in the suburbs, where it is certainly safe for a child to play without finding his mother.

Social Studies Content

Mother is cooking in contemporary stories; she is also cooking in social studies textbooks about cave life. Daddy is also out working (shooting animals?) in those days. In the more modern stories, Daddy comes driving home in his red car. The children run out to greet him. "Daddy works. Daddy works and Bobby works. Bobby works at school and Mother works at home."

In a social studies textbook, the children are shown pictures of persons in various occupations.(55)   Each group consists of three white and two black persons. The text says: "Here are some clothes that tell us what kind of work people do. Look at the pictures and see if you can tell what kind of work these people do." The nurses are *all female;* the doctors are *all male.* In current discussions about unisex clothing, it has been said that it is too confusing for middle America: You don't want to mistake a man for a woman for the same reason that you don't want to mistake the chairman of the board for the janitor. In the textbooks, no such mistakes can be made.

When the textbooks go outside the family and teach about the outer world, the sex stereotyping is the same. The publishers can defend, of course, by saying that they portray the real world as it is. They can't show women in the space program—there are not any. They can't show women on the Supreme Court—there aren't any. An appropriate answer to this would be to point to what happened to the portrayal of black people in the textbooks when the 1966 Federal Executive Order came out saying that there would be no federal money available for textbooks in any school district unless the textbooks were integrated—and showed black people in roles other than porter and maid.

The concessions of the privileged to the unprivileged are seldom brought about by any better motive than the power of the unprivileged to extort them. (J. S. Mill, 1869 [105])

Most money for textbooks comes, directly or indirectly, from the federal government. So, the publishers got busy and blackened faces. This presented all kinds of problems: How can you put black people in the suburbs when they don't live there? Can you portray the typical black person's life in a textbook (it is so lacking in the kinds of niceties which make up the fabric of life shown in textbooks)? These problems were not solved, but were attacked by creating Urban Life series, and also by showing life as it *should* be—that is, integrated.

The point to be made is that when women demand that we be shown in roles other than Mommy baking the cake, it will happen. Until we demand it, we will never be shown as functioning persons in the society, and the young girls will learn, right along with learning to read, that their reading in later years can be confined to cookbooks. No one sat around the Office of Education in 1966 and said, "I think there is a bad image of black people in the textbooks. All black children will grow up thinking they must be domestic servants." The change came because black people themselves developed a bit of self-love and demanded that their children be given fair treatment in the public school reading materials.

Another area of unfairness to women in textbooks is that we are effectively written out of history. It is obvious that because of being constantly pregnant (there was no contraception until recently) and mainly because of the oppressive culture that has kept women down, women have not "made" history to as great an extent as men. (The women Presidents of the United States have not been kept out of the history books; they don't exist.) In addition, there has been a tendency, because men run political systems (and also write history) to value the kinds of contributions which men make and devalue the kinds of contributions which women make. Nonetheless, women have played many important roles in history, and these are missing from the textbooks. For example, an American history textbook contains one paragraph (two sentences) on the woman suffrage movement in the United States.

Reading about Differences

If it is dangerous for little girls to read about Mother who is always in the kitchen cooking (and never in the world being an architect or doctor or plumber), if it is dangerous for little girls to read stories about heroes, with never a heroine—the most harmful of all is for them to read about how young boys and young girls do different things, even at age three.

In an exclusive nursery school in Washington, D. C., parents are told, during their initial tour, about the fine equipment. They are shown the playroom for the little boys: space suits, construction equipment, and mathematical toys. The playroom for little girls contains toy stoves, toy irons, and dolls.

In the textbooks, the boys take the initiative. They decide what to play; they are the leaders. They are also more creative. One story shows a boy and a girl walking through the forest. The boy is eagerly looking for new plants; the girl is afraid she will see a snake, and is clutching on to his hand. The standard illustration is of boys *doing* something (climbing, running, investigating) and girls *watching* them, sometimes silently and sometimes with enthusiasm (the forerunner of the cheerleader who roots for the football team).

This portrayal in the textbooks actually goes against the research, which shows that until the junior high school level, the females excel in almost everything. At puberty, the boys catch up, and then excel in scholastic skills for the rest of their lives. One explanation of this is that the boys have caught up physically. Another explanation is that at puberty the girls get the message that they aren't supposed to win, and so they stop winning.

A story on class elections, written to teach the democratic process, shows a boy as class president, a girl as class secretary. Another girl says: "Bobby, that isn't fair. I'd like to be president. Everyone should have a chance." But she is elected secretary. (Conscious effort is being made to change this pattern. On October 30, 1970, a new national organization was formed, its first chapter in Syracuse, New York. The Future Politicians of America is to train girls in elementary, junior high, and high school for a role as politicians in school politics, in preparation for college politics and national politics.)

Women in Literature

The oppression of women in the textbook field occurs not only in content, but in form. Just as most school teachers are women, but the administrators are men, a high percentage of editors and writers of children's textbooks are women. But publishing houses are run almost exclusively by men. And this is what they choose to tell young girls about themselves.

An essay by E. Fisher in the *New York Times* investigated books for young children in bookstores and libraries and found "an almost incredible conspiracy of conditioning. Boys' achievement drive is encouraged; girls' is cut off. Boys are brought up to express themselves; girls to please. The general image of the female ranges from dull to degrading to invisible." (45)

She found that (although females comprise 51 percent of the population of the United States) they appear in only 20–30 percent of picture books. There were five times as many males in the titles as females, four times as many boys, men, or male animals pictured as there were females. Animals are males, for the most part. In the veld, it is the female lion who does all the work; in the picture-book world, she doesn't exist.

Fisher points out that things are so bad for women in children's story books that one has to go to the Old Testament for an upgrading of the female:

Only in Noah's Ark does Biblical authority enforce equal representation for males and females. Except for Random House's "Pop-up Noah," which has eliminated Mrs. Noah and does not show animals in equal distribution on the cover—males have a slight edge of course. The wives of Ham, Shem, and

Japheth, present in the Old Testament, were missing from all three children's versions I examined.

. . . The marked absence of females in children's books applies even more strongly to books about blacks. Despite the growing number of children's stories about young black boys, Fisher could only find one about a black girl.

Virginia Woolf pointed out that throughout literature women were shown only in relation to men; this is still true in picture books. (166) Friendship between boys is much touted; friendship between boys and girls is frequent; but friendship between girls gets less attention, despite real life, where young girls spend most of their time with their girl friends.

Fisher says that since there are so few females in the books, one would think they'd be very busy, but such is not the case. "What they do is highly limited." What they do *not* do is more telling. They do not drive cars. They do not work, as women do in this country, as executives (few, but they exist), jockeys, college professors, lawyers, stockbrokers, taxi drivers, steelworkers, and physicians. Girls in the books are passive. They walk, read, or dream.

One exception is *Mommies at Work,* by Eve Merriam. Although it describes mothers who split atoms and are writers, it is highly apologetic, closing with: ". . . all Mommies loving the best of all to be your very own Mommy and coming home to you." (103)

Both the textbooks and the fiction for children show male involvement with things and activities, and female involvement with emotions. Boys balance in the tree; girls watch. Boys fish, boys roll in leaves, boys hang from ropes, boys climb, boys make scientific discoveries, boys plant trees. Girls watch—the activities, and the baby. In a book showing an orchestra of twenty-eight animals, the two females are playing (as usual) the harp and the piano.

Until we female authors, editors, teachers, and parents refuse to perpetuate the myths of ourselves as fawning observers, Mommy will always be at home, or at the very best, she will come home from a job and say she really prefers her role as mother to that of college professor.

V

Are Little Girls Being Harmed by "Sesame Street"?

Jane Bergman

Tokenism has come to "Sesame Street." Since its inception, the much-publicized vanguard heavy of educational programs has educated children in part by its consistent presentation of a world virtually without female people. For a little girl engaged in her own passionate struggle for self-definition, watching "Sesame Street" last year—and even this fall—was like taking lessons in invisibility. Each appearance of a female character in her constricted, stereotyped role was doubly damaging because female characters actually appeared so very rarely.

Partially in response to protest about the program's relentless sexism, "Sesame Street" has added two female characters to the cast—one of them a "mail-lady." What else has changed? Is sexism gone from the "new" "Sesame Street"? Tune in.

Puppets and Cartoons

Puppets play an important role. In the puppet universe last season, when a female appeared—which was seldom—she was almost invariably a strident mother, a hapless, hopelessly vague mother, or a simpering, querulous little girl with pigtails and a squeaky voice.

This season, there have been additions to the heavily male puppet cast, mainly in the group scenes: a lady in an incredible rococo hat waiting for a bus; a pony-tailed cheerleader; a monster-woman named Arlene Frantic who sits with two male monsters on a TV game-show panel, and Sally Screamer, a trembly, hysterical game show contestant who wears—right, an incredible rococo hat.

When my young son heard me mention that there are still almost no female puppet-people on "Sesame Street," he disagreed: "There's that mother, you know."

"Roosevelt Franklin's mother?" I asked. Roosevelt Franklin is an amiably rebellious black boy who, last season, was continuously being chased and cornered by his overbearing mother and forced to say his alphabet. Lately Mom seems to have mellowed—read, become more "feminine"; her new image involves greater cooperation with her son in his triumphs. (She still apparently lives in an apron.)

The subtle shift in Mrs. Franklin's attitude does nothing to improve the pervasive momism of the puppet world, and so we have Grover, a wonderfully helpful monster, recently telling a little man who keeps throwing tangerines away over his shoulder to create beautiful offstage smashing noises: "Is your *mommy* going to be *mad* at *you*!"

The cartoon world is as bad, or worse; it's simply overwhelmingly male. Interspersed throughout each program are often more than ten cartoons, most of them designed to teach reading or number skills. Typically, last season, all were narrated by males and almost all were about males. Sometimes, these days, one or two cartoons on a given day will be introduced or narrated by females or will show a female character; these are brief, and very few have been shown so far. On December 8, a randomly selected day of the "new" season, cartoons were shown 14 times, and *all* were by and about males. How does a little girl conceptualize the idea of woman's absolute nonexistence?

Films

What about the new films? Many deal with such topics as animals or farming or how things are made. The ones about human beings invariably show boys and men as active, competent people who do things, girls and women as placid domestic workers, spectators, or passive objects—often, as human backdrops for stories which are really about such things as the lives of vegetables.

A film repeated often on the "new" "Sesame Street" shows James, a New Mexico Indian boy. He narrates, while we see him walking to the school bus with his two sisters following him. (If one weren't aware of the imperatives of "Sesame Street's" pervasive anti-feminism, the question might logically arise: Why isn't it at least half *their* story?) We see kids running outside after school—boys in the foreground, girls somewhere behind them. In James's home, not surprisingly, sex-role stereotypes are the rule: Mother makes tortillas and serves them to the seated family, and mother and grandmother make necklaces out of corn.

"Real" People

In addition to puppets, cartoons, and films, there are ongoing scenes showing the real people who live on Sesame Street. In typical events involving children, girls have been and still are much more visible than in any of the puppet, cartoon, or film sections: at least half are girls. It seems clear that the generally greater prominence of girls here is directly related to the curious *deadness* of "Sesame Street" children. Basically, what they do is line up and listen, take orders, follow directions, pay attention, and strive, with beautifully programed success, to produce the worshiped *right answer*. In accordance with our cultural stereotypes, such roles must be heavily filled by girls.

Even while occasionally getting more active girls into the live sections, "Sesame Street" frequently blows it. For example, Gordon is seen assembling a team of kids for a basketball game. A few boys run up—none of them exactly Willis Reed, but most of them competent-looking—and, finally, they're joined by one daring smallish girl. Gordon's response is, "Hey! How'd *you* get in here?"

The addition of the two new women to the live adult cast is an apparent attempt to correct last season's objectionable ratio of three men to one woman. Molly the "Mail-lady" was the showpiece, very visible on the first new program, not very visible now. (A recent scene in which Bob delivers a package has him mentioning that he is acting *for* Molly, but she never appears.)

Maria, the other newcomer, is much better integrated into the life of the program; it's good to have her there. But it must be emphasized that the change is largely undercut by the addition to the cast of at least *four* new men, actually setting the balance at seven men to three women, and by the appearance, on any given program, of several men but only one woman. The result: Females are, consistently, heavily under-represented in terms of actual air time—just as they were on the "old" "Sesame Street."

At least as significant, the old sexist stereotypes are alive and well. A recent sequence shows the charming monster Grover falling in love with Maria at his first meeting with her. She arrives, and he is transfixed, after the manner of swains through the centuries; his mouth falls open, he sighs wildly, he becomes entirely hysterical trying to anticipate and fill all her requests. Breathless, feverish Grover is practicing chivalry, a behavior which reduces the adored female to an object; she is, in effect, told, "Your wish is my command—so sit still." Grover is ingenuously explicit about the cause of his passion: "OHHHH, she is so *pret-ty*." So much for Maria, the ex-person.

Then there's Susan, the one woman who "integrated" last season's male cast, a determinedly cheerful homemaker notable for her impeccable posture. Susan is still the quintessential housewife, spending her days in mindless domestic service: shopping for oranges (she counts them with the kids), endlessly icing homemade cakes and serving juices and hanging balloons for kids' parties, or just posing with a laundry basket or in front of her dishtowel and refrigerator—and always with this highly inappropriate smile on her face. (It has been mentioned on the program that Susan once did have a vocation. She was a nurse—what else, a surgeon? Now she simply looks neat, devotes herself to others, stays home, needs nothing—and never, never *does* anything.)

Perpetuation of Stereotypes

All in all, "Sesame Street" *has* changed, from being incredibly sexist to being slightly less sexist. And *that's* what we used to call tokenism.

I have the impression that originally the program was put together in part with an eye toward upgrading the image of men for the benefit of black children who have had small opportunity to see brothers or fathers functioning in the world with autonomy and self-respect. Even if this be true, there can be no justification for the creation of a program for black *and* white boys *and* girls full of such vicious, relentless sexism.

With exquisite verisimilitude, the program shows little girls that, in our culture, being female is being nobody. It is also a fact that black people were once literal slaves. Would black parents object if "Sesame Street's" blacks—not all, just almost all—were fat, kerchiefed mammies and cotton-picking, shuffling Uncle Toms?

As a feminist, I am engaged in an effort to make our home a place where sexist stereotypes will not be perpetuated, where our children can feel free to learn about becoming not aggressively "masculine" or passively "feminine," as defined by a hideous cultural stereotype, but human. For my husband and me, it is very much an ongoing struggle with our own conditioning, and we are trying, always, to make whole people out of the male and female puppets we once felt ourselves to be. For our daughter, we want a life truly full of the joy of knowing herself to be *real*. We want her to have a continuing sense of the options involved in self-definition.

Watching "Sesame Street" this season I had too many moments when the only appropriate response seemed to be to turn off the set.

Hey! "Sesame Street"! Is *that* the right answer?

VI

Down the Up Staircase: Sex Roles, Professionalization, and the Status of Teachers

Barbara Heyns

The growth of the professions has been one of the most remarkable and remarked upon aspects of the occupational structure during the last thirty years. The census category "Professional, Technical, and Kindred Workers" increased nearly 100 percent between 1950 and 1965, and the trend shows every sign of continuing.(82) The reasons most frequently given are the increased demand for specialized expertise and technical competence, and the growing fund of scientific knowledge underpinning expertise. Concurrently, the status, income, and organizational power of professional groups have grown immeasurably. Professionalization can be seen in the expanding influence of the traditional professions, as well as in the claims and aspirations of less well established occupations. (For an excellent discussion of the profession of teaching, see R. Dreeben. [39])

The characteristics which are typically used to differentiate a profession from other vocations consist of both prerogatives and responsibilities. In general, professionals perform essential social services, requiring intellectual skills and techniques developed through a relatively prolonged period of specialized training. Professionals deal with clients, rather than customers, and are accountable to colleagues, rather than clientele. A code of professional ethics and standards guides practitioners, who enjoy relative autonomy in performing their services. To the extent that a profession is highly organized and monopolizes the delivery of particular services, control over recruitment and training institutions, as well as credentials and licensing requirements, is widespread. High levels of compensation and related benefits for professionals are also typical. Occupations which are highly professionalized, such as medicine, exhibit all these characteristics, while those in the process of professionalizing tend to be remiss in several. Professionalization is often viewed as a form of collective social mobility; the more professionalized the occupational group the higher the status of the members.

Status of Teachers

The status of teaching at elementary and secondary levels typically ranks lower than most other professions. Increasing the status of the profession has often been singled out as one of the most important remedies for an ailing educational enterprise. The argument is basically that if teachers were more professional, education standards would be higher and better schools would result. Higher salaries in conjunction with increased prestige would attract more dedicated and effective teachers than are now available. Greater autonomy would allow for more curricular innovation and larger amounts of individualized attention. Quite often, the organization of schools imposes constraints on the teacher's ability to do more than adhere to a rigid and inflexible schedule and insure, through discipline if necessary, that students do the same.

The arguments for professionalization in education in at least those dimensions which affect autonomy and working conditions seem compelling. The concern at present is the logic of perceived obstacles to professionalization rather than the ultimate rationale. If teaching and teachers have been "bypassed by the professional revolution," (89) as many critics maintain, one is forced to question how this came about, and in what respects it may be changing. Three interrelated aspects of the teaching profession are the focus at present: the proportion female, salary levels, and the impotence of professional organizations. Advocates of professionalization tend to argue that changes in each of these are required in order to increase the status of teachers.

Historical Background

Teaching as a profession is unique in many respects. It is first a woman's profession, and this is generally seen as both a cause and a consequence of the inferior status it is accorded. Historically, it was the only profession truly open to women and the major outlet for the talents and energies of those first few women who fought for the right to pursue higher education. Seventy percent of the graduates of Mt. Holyoke during its first forty years became elementary and secondary teachers.(115) Women such as Catharine Beecher were instrumental in establishing schools and in training and enlisting many young teachers, often for distant frontier communities. The schoolmarm committed to educating and civilizing the West did far more than marry the sheriff—Hollywood notwithstanding.

By 1870, women constituted the majority of all teachers, and the profession has remained predominately female to this day. (44; 89) At the turn of the century, 70 percent of all teachers were women and 85 percent of all professional women were teachers. Despite such numerical predominance, salary schedules invariably favored male teachers at every level. In fact, Michael Katz has argued that the feminization of education was primarily accomplished for reasons of economy; the most efficient method of educating the expanding population of poor immigrants without increasing the tax burden was to replace male teachers with female ones. (83) (A similar argument is advanced by L. R. Harlan. [63])

Sex Roles in Teaching

Sex roles have traditionally been assumed to play a major role in the choice of teaching as a profession. Teaching allowed the more nurturant and maternal qualities of the feminine personality free rein, while not requiring excessive commitment to the profession. The popular mystique attributes both great patience and a temperament suited to fulfilling the needs of young children to womanhood. Teaching schedules tend to dovetail perfectly with those of children, allowing mothers the ideal arrangement for managing both primary obligations and secondary commitments. A teaching credential permits an intermittent career, with opportunities for geographic mobility. As M. Lieberman so succinctly states the case:

The woman teacher interested chiefly in marriage and a home is not likely to take a strong interest in raising professional standards and in improving the conditions of teaching. Indeed, such women are frequently opposed to raising professional standards; such action runs contrary to their personal long term interests. (89)

The question at issue is whether female teachers are in fact less professional than male teachers, not whether they must be because they are women. Males in education are generally more eager to leave teaching than are females, are less satisfied, and have fewer concerns with improving standards.(35; 98)   Female teachers typically score higher on scales of professionalism than do males, even when compared only to men planning to stay in education, according to J. L. Colombotos.(26)   He found that married women were more family-oriented than single teachers. Family-oriented women teachers, however, were also more professional than males, perhaps due to the increased commitment necessary to keep them in education. Colombotos concludes that "these data suggest a reexamination of the common assumption that women's family roles inhibit the development of professionalism on the job." Such a reexamination is long overdue.

Salaries

The levels of compensation offered by teaching are also construed as both a reason for and a result of lesser professionalization. Teaching has never been a profession in which expectations of amassing great wealth or renown were particularly high. The salaries of teachers have been, and are now, lower than those offered to persons with similar education and job experience, even when taking into account the seasonal nature of employment. The National Education Association argued recently that by accepting substandard salaries, teachers could be viewed as personally underwriting one eighth of the cost of public education. (44) Although education is widely considered one of the few professions in which salary scales are identical for men and women, male teachers still receive more income than women with comparable amounts of experience.* While teaching is often a stepping stone to an administrative position for a male, such career contingencies are infrequently accessible to women. The lifetime earnings of women teachers are therefore more tied to the less lucrative potentiality offered by seniority. Men tend to be concentrated in districts as well as grade levels and specialities which pay more. The football coach typically receives larger benefits and extra funds for "coaching" which the woman teacher does not receive, however much time she may spend with the Glee Club.

Income differentials, however, probably do contribute to the greater attractiveness of the profession for women than for men. The "opportunity costs" associated with teaching for men are substantially greater than for women. Between 1950 and 1960, the rate of increase of teachers' salaries was similar to the rate for all professionals; salaries of female teachers, however, grew relatively more quickly than salaries of all professional women, while the salaries of male teachers grew less rapidly. (46) A common fear expressed by advocates of professionalization is that the salaries of women in education retard income gains for everyone and function to maintain the existing imbalance in the sex ratio. In fact, the proportion of males teaching increased during the same decade, and it is extremely doubtful that the incentive of a military deferment was operating at that time. While it is often argued that the surest method of enticing more males into teaching is to offer higher salaries, this seems most undesirable. Women entered and dominated the profession not because it offered lower salaries, but because there were, and are, few alternatives. The status of teachers will not improve, ipso facto, when more males enter the profession.

*Personal communication from the NEA.

Improvements will come when competent teachers, gender aside, are provided with more favorable conditions in which to teach.

Teacher Organizations

Several authorities have argued that a principal means of upgrading the status of teachers is augmenting and centralizing the organizations which represent teachers. Obstacles to such efforts include the decentralized control of educational employment, high turnover rates, and the difficulties in organizing "women's occupations." The notion implicit in the final obstacles is either that women *per se* cannot be organized, or that decentralized control and high turnover rates characterize occupations in which women are concentrated. The latter is clearly true; however, in education, administrative control is typically in the hands of a male educator, who chooses not to identify with professional organizations and often exerts little effort to improve the general lot of teachers. Women have not been involved in professional organizations to the same extent as men, yet the assertion that this is due to lower amounts of professional concern seems dubious.

The sex ratio in teaching clearly influences the profession, and there arc legitimate reasons why more men would be desirable in teaching. If male teachers were actually able to improve the reading scores and reduce the misbehavior of little boys, that alone could be sufficient justification. Women teachers, on the average, seem much less concerned about increasing the proportion of males than do men teachers and are understandably reluctant to endorse differential pay scales at their own expense. (159) Balancing the sex ratio in many different aspects of social life seems necessary, but a myopic concentration on education tends to distort the logic. As professional opportunities for women expand, the concentration of women in education will no doubt decrease. What is needed, however, is not greater incentive for men, but more alternatives for women.

The most recent developments in professional militancy tend to make many arguments for strong teachers' organizations rather obsolete. Highly successful strikes, orchestrated by teachers' unions, show more promise of increasing the power, status, and most especially the salaries of teachers than any other happening to date. What is rather disconcerting is to observe that the first serious evaluations of the reasons leap to the conclusion that male teachers are responsible, because the increase in militancy has been concurrent with an increasing proportion of men in the profession. R. C. Williams argues, for example, that the

change from a female- to a male-dominated profession has had an enormous impact on the evolution of teacher militancy. . . . Teaching has been considered traditionally a feminine role. Male teachers are expected to play a subservient role to administrators and school boards; male teachers work in one of the few occupations where there is no financial discrimination against women; male teachers do what society considers a woman's job and they are paid a woman's salary for it. (160)

Such conjectures require more substantiation than conventional myth, particularly in a period in which women are increasingly objecting to their traditional social and occupational roles. In a highly interesting study of militant professionalism, R. G. Corwin found that the more professional the teacher in orientation, the more likely he or she was to be militant. (27) The relationship was positive for both sexes, but more pronounced for women teachers. Although males typically scored higher in militancy, the differences were considerably reduced when age was introduced as a control. Such findings do not refute the assumption that males were instrumental in promoting militancy; they do, however, indicate that sex interacts with age.

The most startling change in the demographic composition of teachers between 1961 and 1971 was not the change in proportion female, from 68.7 percent to 65.7 percent, but the age and experience levels of female teachers. In 1961, the median age of women teachers was 45.5 compared to a median of 33.6 for males. In 1971, the respective median ages were 37 and 33. The median years of experience for males and females was equal in 1971, at eight years. This represented an increase for males from 7.1 years experience in 1961, while females declined from a high of 14.2 years experience. Perhaps these changes in composition had more influence on militancy than the changing sex ratio. The conclusion that young teachers of both sexes were critical to increases in militancy is somewhat speculative; however, it deserves consideration.

Conclusion

In summary, this chapter has attempted to discredit prevalent notions regarding the profession of teaching. There is evidence which suggests that women in teaching tend to be more professional in their orientations than are men teachers. While high rates of teacher turnover may constitute a hurdle to professionalization, female teachers are not the worst offenders. Compensation in teaching is quite low, and this is probably related to the disproportionate numbers of women in the field. Raising salaries for males, however, would seem to be an inappropriate solution. Teacher militancy seems related to sex, age, and professionalism; it is facile to conclude, however, that the sexual composition of the profession was largely responsible for increased militancy.

The central argument bears repeating. The status of teachers is intrinsically linked to the status of professional women. To the degree that opportunities for equitable compensation exist in many sectors of the economy, the energies of women will become less focused on teaching, and the profession will be less dominated by women. "Education," asserts Lieberman, "will not become a leading profession unless the proportion of men to women is drastically increased or there occurs a cultural revolution concerning the status of women."(89)   I would argue that both are necessary, and that they will occur together or not at all.

Part Three
Higher Education

In the lower grades of teaching men have almost ceased to compete with women; in the higher grade, that is, in college teaching, women are just beginning to compete with men, and this competition is beset with the bitterest jealousy that women have ever had to meet . . . on account of this jealousy college presidents and boards of trustees (all of whom are, as a rule, men) cannot, even if they would, materially add to the number of women teachers or advance them.

M. C. Thomas
"Should the Higher Education
of Women Differ from that of Men?"
1901

VII

Some Dilemmas
of Women's Education

David Riesman

I want to discuss women in higher education and some of the problems and prospects that face women as they go on in college and university studies in this country. And I want to begin by describing the "minority" status of women, that peculiar minority who are not numerically such, but who still remain, in spite of all that is said about "momism" and so on, a somewhat oppressed group.

Minority Status

One of the "peculiarities" of this minority is that it is brought up by persons of the same sex: not only do girls have women for their mothers, but their early teachers are likely to be women. Women are on to each other's tricks, and at the same time have a certain sympathy for each other. In consequence, since girls are faced by *doyennes* in school and at home, they are apt to be less rebellious than boys. Boys, in fact, faced by teachers of the opposite sex, often feel that they must rebel in order to consider themselves truly boys. To be sure, girls sometimes feel under very great pressure precisely because they are being controlled by members of their own sex, and they can be rebellious, but our society on the whole will put up with less rebellion from girls than from boys. For example, women students drop out with less than the ease now available to young men in many of our very best institutions. Something like 20 percent of the Harvard College undergraduates drop out and return at some point;

Reprinted from *Educational Record* (Fall 1965): 424-434, by permission of the American Council on Education.

they leave and drive a truck, or join the Peace Corps, or go to San Francisco, or enter the Army for a year or two, and then come back. Young women, if they drop out of college for nonacademic reasons, are apt to do so to get married. And by the same token, they are well advised to remain in college until they get their first degrees, in order to be sure that they have a certain amount of education before being caught up in matrimony. Hence, for a variety of reasons, the orbits of girls are generally narrower than those of boys at every stage.

But there is another peculiarity about girls: from their early days of school they are more people-oriented than boys. They are more adept at the social side of life, and they have fewer distractions from it, whether in sports, or hotrodding, or science fiction, or many other things which are not exclusively, but largely, boys' hobbies.

To put this in context, let me present the utopia that I would like to see in which girls would not be discriminated against in education or elsewhere. This would be a world in which the actual biocultural distinctions between the sexes would be seen as large, overlapping curves in which many boys would be in their temperaments more like most girls than like most boys; and so, too, with girls—the differences would be group differences that would permit individuals to pursue their own native endowment irrespective of sex. Girls have sometimes felt confined by such a recognition of the differences which may exist between any large group of women and any large group of men—differences which are, I think, almost universal (although Margaret Mead, I am sure, could find a society in which they are not evident). For instance, if girls are told that boys are better at certain physical activities, girls may resent this as a constriction. At the same time, it may be comforting, and even liberating, for girls to learn that what they might otherwise regard as failure in competition with boys reflects differences which are not necessarily to be regarded invidiously—although people in our society are almost always apt to assume that, if there are differences among people, these imply a relation of superiority and inferiority.

In psychological terms, I think there is some very arguable evidence that girls are more receptive than boys, and that boys are more performance-oriented; if so, this may reflect their sex roles, where girls' sexual performance is invisible and boys' visible. Erik Erikson in a paper in *Daedalus* on the woman in America shows that boys and girls very early have different configurations in play. (42) Boys are likely to build taller buildings (which fall down more often). Girls are likely to build houses and create a more domestic setting, and this occurs even before these differences are fully conscious. But this does not mean that in my utopia *all* girls must be receptive or *all* boys performance-oriented.

Solidarity Among Women

Except in *Lysistrata* and in the suffragette movement* there is generally very little solidarity among women as a minority. Indeed, one can often hear women say that they prefer the company of men. Usually this means that they do not like mannish women; also they are saying of themselves "I am terribly female." One no longer finds Negroes saying that they don't like other Negroes, although it is often true. But in the particular minority of women this lack of solidarity can still be expressed, and, in fact, in many situations in our national life women are their own worst enemies. For instance, when women are in business, they do not like to work for other women. In contrast, it is almost impossible to find men saying that they do not like other men in the way that it remains quite legitimate for a woman to say she doesn't like women. And in many fields of our national life, as in engineering, in medicine except for a few specialties, in law, in university life, or in hunting, men are living a stag life; they never say they do not like men. Moreover, it is difficult for women to have a "union" against men because they are all tied to, or hope to be tied to, specific men. They cannot unite against the oppressor, let us say, in the way the Black Muslims unite against the white race, or the French Canadians in Quebec against the English, because at every point they are related to a man, whether he is their father or their boyfriend. This is even true of sisters in a convent or a mother house where Brides of Christ are the "subjects" of bishops (and, as John Cogley noted in a discussion in *The Commonweal,* are subject to man-made canon law).

This does not mean, of course, that women are powerless. No minority is ever wholly powerless. In the countries where men are even more dominant than they are in America—that is, in Latin America, or in Italy, or in Spain, or in the Arab countries—women can compel men to fight other men over a woman's honor. It is a terrific power that can get men to kill each other. Women can manipulate men more subtly in our own society. But in general, women are suspicious of each other, as the urban poor and peasants tend to be suspicious of each other—in general, oppressed groups have little solidarity.

One might ask: Why should there be solidarity among women? Turn the question around. What are some of the oppressions in an academic environment that women suffer from?

The "Male" Mode

I think what is happening in American academic life is an increasing shift toward a metaphorically "male" mode of

---

*Ed. note: It is important to remind the reader that this paper was first published in 1965—before the women's liberation "movement" was as widespread as it is today and before Vassar became coed.

performance. I am speaking here only of the leading high-pressure institutions which demand top performance, which insist on purposefulness in terms of college as preparation for graduate work, which are driving out intellectual pleasure for its own sake just as they are driving out the lowbrow "collegiate." What is happening in our major educational institutions today is that, on the one hand, the kind of frivolity characteristic of the collegiate is being more and more pushed aside and left to the high schools to exploit, while, on the other hand, what might be called the "higher frivolity" of intellectual work or academic work pursued for its own joy is also being driven out by academic pressurefulness. In our major universities we appear to be moving toward a meritocracy in which the boys have learned to work "for the record" before coming to college and even starting in the sixth grade. College itself becomes something for the record, whether preparatory training for the job or for graduate school. Boys work toward a goal which is not the goal of learning and, as I see among my own students, find it difficult to get interested in one subject because it would distract them from a fair apportioning of their "investments" in all subjects. They take, so to speak, the attitude of bankers toward their time and energy while they are still in college.

But it is not only in this sense of purposefulness that our institutions are becoming "male," in quotation marks—in the sense of being pointed toward the sort of career line which is specifically male, or very largely male. It is also "male" in the kinds of abstractions which are increasingly favored in our intellectual life. Our academic disciplines become related, not to the world outside, not to what is concrete, but to each other and to their own internal development. For instance, one finds in the social sciences in our major universities that many girls enter, let us say, a psychology class, because, as I said earlier, they are natural sociometrists—they are interested in people. Nothing is so infuriating to many male professors of psychology as to have a girl in his course for this reason. And he soon makes clear to her that psychology has nothing whatsoever to do with human beings! And he tries to kick her out because she won't become his disciple. The same is true, though perhaps to a somewhat lesser degree, of sociology, which in many universities is a girls' subject because girls want to help people: they are interested in society. And here again the professor makes perfectly clear that sociology has nothing to do with such ordinary everyday issues. Even the professor of English in a big high-pressure university can make clear to his students that the New Criticism has very little to do with the "mere" appreciation of literature. (Of course, a good many women in academic disciplines behave in just this dominant style, sometimes with added "minority" zeal.)

*Reactions to
the "Male" Models*

How do girls react to these "masculine" models when they confront them in the academy? I hope it is clear that in using male and female here in reference to styles of thought I am doing so metaphorically. I am not saying that a particular way of thinking is necessarily inherently male or inherently female, but I am saying (and I know that this is arguable: there are many who disagree with me) that girls in general the world over tend to be more concrete, more down to earth, less abstract, less ideological, less conceptual; and if this were not so, the world might have come to an end long since; the girls have kept things going. And if one wants to pursue this, one can (as Erich Fromm has emphasized) do so in Greek mythology in plays like *Antigone,* which show the struggle between the traditional female world and what was then the new patriarchal society.

Girls react to the male definitions of academia with a good deal of discomfort and ambivalence, as one might expect. They sometimes feel a personal inadequacy, and I often see my own students coming to the conclusion that they lack ability in various fields when, in fact, what they lack is the ability to structure their thinking in the way that men have defined their sphere. Indeed, the way men have defined their spheres is not suitable to many men, because, as I said earlier, we deal in overlapping curves and there are many young men who are as put off, let us say, by male definitions of psychology or sociology or literature as the young women are.

But, as already suggested, there is another women's reaction which is similar to the desire of a backward country to overtake and surpass the leaders. And one often finds in major coeducational universities a rigid conformism among girls as ultra-academic students who read all the readings with an even, undiscriminating diligence. Diana Trilling once put this rather well in an article on Radcliffe in *The Reporter* in which she said that girls, in order to feel they are getting as good an education as boys, must get as bad a one. But another reaction I also find is a rejection of the male-defined subject as inhumane. Thus many girls both in high school and college decide that science—physics, chemistry—is inhumane and that to study these things would somehow de-feminize them. Some of the social sciences, too, perhaps especially economics, may be reacted to in this way at times. I think this is unfortunate, because when rightly taught science is a liberating art like any other and as metaphorical and fluid as some sorts of poetry. But I think it is often taught in such a way as to confirm the feeling that it is inhumane, and because the more humane is driven out of it, the field itself rigidifies.

Another reaction that I find among girl students is learning to play the game as a game. For example, I was at a discussion at Radcliffe last spring when a group of very thoughtful girls were saying that they had discovered pretty well along in their freshman year that the way to get ahead at Harvard was to attack the book and the professor. But they did not like to do this. It was not their natural style. They felt that this mode was a constriction on them; and it was corrosive to play the game, while it was self-defeating not to play it. It was corrosive to play it in that it would deny one's integrity because the model would come from the male students and from the male professor.

There is still another reaction which I find in the major coeducational institutions and also in the kinds of high-powered women's colleges represented by Smith, Wellesley, Mount Holyoke, or Vassar: in football metaphor, a run around end into the arts as an area where women are not at a disadvantage and do not have to submit to male models. In a place like an Ivy League university this is difficult because the arts are taught not from the standpoint of the performing artists, but in a verbal way. One does not teach painting, but art history. One does not teach music, but musicology. So there is something missing in the arts in the male-dominated environment (in the metaphorical sense that I am using "male"). And again I want to emphasize that men suffer from arbitrary sex-role definitions no less than women, because every boundary that says "this is women's work or women's way" is also a statement "this is not men's work, this is not men's way." So men also are limited and cut off by every male device of oppression. (I think, in general, one sees in any society that any group that oppresses another group is bounded and limited by that oppression.)

Women, Careers, and Marriage

However, I want to make clear that I am not saying that people are becoming more narrow and more specialized. Indeed, students *are* under pressure to become more narrow and more specialized; but I am very much pleased with the ability of young people to resist that pressure in many different ways. For instance, I have seen many people from excellent colleges go into the Peace Corps, where even an amateur can make a contribution, and be a person of importance, just as in schoolteaching many make a contribution here within the United States.

Girls, on the other hand, have difficulty in specializing in terms of high academic performance because they sometimes fear that this will narrow their marriage market. They fear, for one thing, that by the time they are through academic training, all the "good" men will be taken, and they get into a panic in their fourth year in college if they are already twenty-one and not pinned. At the same time, many young women in college are aware that if they have not formed themselves as human beings and as intellectually and professionally competent women prior to marriage, the chances of seeking out and holding onto a genuine sense of intellectual commitment after marriage becomes considerably more difficult. If women drop out of college to marry, or, after completing two years of junior college, do not continue their education, they may not always reach the point where they can, after their children have grown and flown, come back to work at a sufficiently professional level. One might refer to this view of the staging of women's careers as a "back of the stove" theory of women's education in which women after college keep the pot of their intellectual life simmering on the back burner while the children are in their early years, so that they are ready to bring it quickly to a boil when the children are a bit older.

Certain careers for women are limited because they can be pursued only in a few places, and because men may not be at those places. Historically, in our society, a wife can be "ill," in quotation marks, she can be neurotically ill, she can be extravagant, she can drive her husband to death, but she cannot consciously subordinate her husband's career aims to hers. Consider a girl who wants to finish graduate training and whose husband is living in a place where no such training is available; such a girl would feel rotten if she forced her husband to move away from his career line in order to advantage hers. In other words, a woman, as I have said, can be ailing conveniently, or be extravagant conveniently, and society will put up with her; but if she puts her career aims even on a parity with her husband's, she is in difficulty.

But beyond that there is a terrible fear among college girls that to be obviously brighter than one's spouse is dangerous. It is perfectly all right, in fact not only all right but desirable, that a girl be better looking than her husband. Sometimes she can beat him at tennis. If she is a Negro, she should be lighter skinned, at least until very recently. If her husband is successful, she could be of higher social class. But she cannot be much more obviously brilliant and talented. And yet graduate school is where the men are and especially those who might allow their prospective wives a wider orbit; thus a girl is often torn between two alternatives: if she goes on to graduate school, she becomes more differentiated and therefore fears men will reject her; on the other hand, if she does not go there, where will she find men up to her level?

And, of course, one of the problems bright girls have is the same problem that a girl six foot tall has, which is that six foot men marry girls who are five foot two. And many boys of six-foot-six intellect marry girls of four-foot-two intellect. So the bright girl fears she has a narrow market.

What Educational Institutions Can Do

What can be done? What are some of the things that our society and our educational institutions might do so that they would handicap women less than I think they now do and consequently handicap men less? In the long run, what I would like to see is a turnover in our educational system in terms of sex balance. I would like to see men teaching in elementary school and teaching the arts in secondary school, not only science and physical education. I would like to see many more women teaching in our major universities, especially in the sciences. I would like to see our universities at the faculty level as well as at the student level create a less sex-typed culture in which there is more ready give-and-take and in which women's ways of looking at phenomena would be encouraged as well as the abstract conceptual ways favored by the dominant men, although not by all men.

This would require thinking of our educational system less in terms of manpower for social utility (which I think in a rich society, or a potentially rich one, is less and less necessary) and more in terms of human quality and human potential. One can observe, on committees deciding on graduate fellowships, that there is a tendency, where a girl and a boy have relatively equal records, to choose the boy, on the ground that he is a better bet for manpower since he is not likely to drop out because of marriage. And therefore he will serve the society and the professor himself as a disciple. My own feeling is that society can afford to and should educate women to the limit of their bents without excessive worry about what they will do with it. If they want to use their minds as homemakers and reflective readers without any "production" ever coming from it, I think that should suffice. If they want then to change their minds and do something later, that is fine. Women should be free to do this without having to incur a judgment at some point, in college or later, whether they will add to the national manpower in a supposedly undersupplied field. We do not know what fields are really needed by our society. We do not know what a rich society like our needs because no society has achieved sufficient abundance to present such a puzzling challenge.

We also need enormously greater flexibility for part-time study and part-time work for women. As Everett Hughes likes to point out, men work part time too. They spend eight hours at the office and then come home to their wives and complain about the busy day they have had, but if you actually analyze, through a time-and-motion study, the work they have done at the office, you would see that a lot of it was sociability—"conferences," getting their plane tickets, and so on. Many women who work four hours *really* work and put out much more than the men who are at it eight hours. But our society calls the women's work part time and the men's work full time, and we have insufficient place and flexibility for the part time. There are many graduate institutions which will not allow people to take degrees part time, a tacit form of discrimination, which is hard on married women and on working wives.

We need also to get rid of the assumption that is so dominant in many fields that one must make one's mark by a certain age. In mathematics, for instance, supposedly one shows one's ability by the age of twenty or so. The physicist is said to be an old man by the time he is thirty. But, in fact, these judgments tend to be self-confirming. I was talking to a colleague in physics at Harvard last spring who said that the age of entering graduate students in physics has been dropping steadily until now it is around twenty or twenty-one, cutting out people who have done other things and have come back to school. It would certainly cut out women who have stopped to have a family and then come back to school.

But in order to make it possible for the woman who comes back to catch up, we need, in a curious and paradoxical way, more abstraction rather than less. That is, we need the field to be seen in a much more imaginative way so that one does not have to plow through it in a factual way to grasp what has happened in the interim. When I talk to women who have been out, who are now, let us say, in their thirties, and who want to come back and continue their graduate work to prepare for a career rather than just a job, they all say, "I have missed so much of the literature." But actually they would not be so put off by this if they had ways of then overtaking and surpassing which did not require plowing through all the literature that has been in the meantime disproved. I sometimes say to them, when they say they have missed all the literature, that they are lucky to have missed most of it.

These returning women need refresher courses which will help them do this abstracting job, and they need foundations and other agencies to give them fellowships so that they can return at this point, and they need programs of counseling, such as the Sarah Lawrence Center for Continuing Education.

Security for the Men

But I think before one can ask for these things for women, one has to work on the men and give them a greater security, because many of the constrictions from which women suffer in our society come from men's anxiety. Men cannot stand the competition of women in addition to the competition of their own sex, and men need a kind of social insurance against the threats to their masculinity which they see in emancipated women.

I think what I would ideally like to see in our society is that sex become an ascribed rather than an achieved status—that one is simply born a girl or a boy and that is it. And no worry about an activity's de-feminizing or emasculating one, as the case might be, according to how the culture presently sex-types particular ways of behaving. In our society, in part because we are a democracy, we have few ascribed statuses. We are not born a lord or a peasant, and in the same way, ironically, we are not born male or female. We have to achieve maleness or femaleness over and over again.

And if there is to be greater security among men, there also must be a greater "live and let live" attitude among women toward other women who choose a different road. If you have ever been in a discussion or ever have the chance to be in a discussion in which women who are pursuing careers are with women who, in their own phrase, are "just housewives," you may conclude that the bitterness of such a confrontation springs from the insecurity of both groups. The "just-housewives" feel that they let their college education down, that in a performance-oriented society they are performing in a very narrow sphere, although they can certainly "perform" there and make their children perform on their behalf in ways that are terrifying. And the women who are pursuing careers feel guilty because they may not be lavishing on their children or on their families all the energy that the housewives can muster. Thus the confrontation makes both groups insecure and both groups attack each other, and this I would like to see moderated.

Still a Man's World

But it would require long-run social developments. What can be done now? One of the less drastic things that can be done is to develop a better sense of the issues I have been discussing, to get a better sense of what are the inevitable limitations put on women in what I think is still a man's world in many areas. However, one should also learn to recognize the bounties of living in a man's world, for there are many indulgences granted to women. These latter are not unmixed blessings because what they may mean is that a girl does not feel she has to drive herself toward a long-run goal, and if she is not anxious to achieve, she may also not be developing fully because she feels she can take it easy—she has another way out; she can always get married.

It is not news that girls have an unquenchable interest in the world of boys. I have never found, for instance, a girl who did not want to read *Lord of the Flies,* because it is a boy's book and there is not a girl in it (although I think that some of the miasma that I find in the book derives from that very fact). Girls are very eager to read *Catcher in the Rye,* which is largely a boy's book. There is no female ethnocentrism about women's world, and I would be surprised if more than a handful of women in any audience will have read Virginia Woolf's *A Room of One's Own,* which is a girl's book. When a student of mine at Radcliffe did her honors thesis on "Freshman Attitudes at Radcliffe," she asked girls what was important, and they said "Study is important, dates are important, other girls take second place." If there is a conflict between a date and another girl, the other girl is canceled out, by a kind of mutual consent. If there is a conflict between study and another girl, this is a difficulty and the other girl tends to drop to second place there, too.

And yet for girls to gain a more differentiated picture of the man's world is not enough. They must also learn something about their own, and it is liberating, I think, for girls to sort out the personal obstacles from the social barriers that they suffer from and take advantage of as women. There are, as I have suggested, what the psychiatrists might call secondary gains to belonging to the oppressed minority—the female sex. There is less need to make money and to do other distasteful things. There is more possibility, if not more need, to discover one's own interests because there is less immediate economic imperative—not universally so, but often.

Women in Science

I have argued that science in high school and often in college presents itself in a way that drives girls off. The "male" presentation may reflect a need to order the universe around rather than listening to it "with the third ear." A very interesting psychological experiment put college students in the following situation. (163) They were placed in a tilting chair in a tilting room and asked either to make the chair upright with gravity in the tilting room or to make the room upright with the tilting chair. Boys could do this better than girls. The boys were less distracted by the surrounding set than the girls were. The boys were more independent of the field, as the psychologist would put it, in a social as well as a physical setting. This is usually put to the credit of boys. They are said to be more independent, less field-dependent. But this is a "male" description of the result. One could also say that the male is less aware of the immediate situation he is in, and needs order above response.

And as I have also argued, I would like to see more women in science, not only for the sake of the many women who could do talented work but for the sake of science, because it would present a different face to society if the women in it were sufficiently numerous and confident not to follow the male models or definitions. These are very subtle matters, as you realize, and one would have to detail the sociology of particular sciences and particular fields to show how maleness and femaleness operate in these fields to define standard performance. In anthropology, for example, one would have to ask why subtle and responsive field work, at which women are excellent, may count less than, let us say, elegant work on kinship systems, at which men are rather good.

A Look at Other Societies

Here I think we can get some help from looking at other societies and at the subsocieties within our own society. Upper-class women in

America have somewhat more freedom. Recall Amy Lowell and her cigar and her assertiveness as an upper-class woman. But on the whole, women in America, even in the upper class, are constantly asked, in effect, "Who do you think you are?" when they are bold and assertive, with the result that if they continue to be bold and assertive, they tend almost in a self-confirming vicious circle to become, by American definition, unfeminine.

One might ask why it is that European career women seem more feminine than American career women. Perhaps European men are less threatened and therefore European career women, who are frequently upper class, are able to continue their development without having to go through the sound barrier, so to speak, as one would have to in this country against so much opposition. In the lower social strata in Europe, career women might meet quite a lot of objection. But it is more important in Europe that one is upper class than that one is a woman. (If one reads Simone de Beauvoir's *Memoirs of a Dutiful Daughter,* one can get some sense of this.) And one sees in these European women that it is possible to be assertive and yet feminine and womanly.

To be sure, women in Europe and in other parts of the world also often have a harder time than men in pursuing higher education, and it is not only in the United States that many women feel, if they pursue intellectual aims, that they may become incapable of "giving," of being truly female. Often without full consciousness of what they are doing, men and many women have set up the game that way. It is important to become skeptical of these time-bound and parochial definitions about what is important in life, what is good performance, and what is supposedly characteristic of men and of women. Individual women may then, in the short run, without becoming martyrs or fighting the old feminist crusades of a generation ago, take advantage of the point to which that crusade has brought women. In most parts of our society, it is now unquestioned that it is as legitimate for women to go to college as men, even if they are not outstanding or particularly accomplished academically. In the short run also, individual women can take advantage of knowing better what being female means for their intellectual development and whether it puts any boundaries of a specific sort on it or not; while, in the long run, one can only hope and work for greater freedom for both sexes so that men, less anxious, will allow women to develop their potential.

VIII

The Effect
of Race and Sex
on College Admission

Elaine Walster, T. Anne Cleary,
and Margaret M. Clifford

Whether being black is an advantage or disadvantage for a college applicant is more debatable at present than it might have been a few years ago. The increased college enrollment of blacks has been perceived by some as a reduction of racial bias, but others have seen it as a change in the direction of the bias. There is certainly less controversy regarding the effect of sex on college admission; most observers agree that it is a handicap to be a woman. However, we have no experimental evidence regarding the effect of race and sex.

This experiment was designed to test the hypothesis that both race and sex affect a candidate's likelihood of being admitted to college. Assuming that most colleges are anxious to increase the representativeness of their student bodies, and mindful that many are actively recruiting competent black scholars, we predicted that a black candidate, male or female, would be preferred to a comparable white candidate. Furthermore, whether the candidate was black or white, it was predicted that sex would also affect an applicant's chance of admission, with preference given to male candidates.

The design of the experiment was a simple one. Applications for admission should be identical in all respects, except the race and sex of the applicant must be randomly varied. One quarter of the time the applicant should be said to be a black male, a black female, a white male, or a white female. Whether the applicant is accepted or rejected

Reprinted from *Sociology of Eduction, 44* (Spring 1970), 237-244, by permission of The American Sociological Association.

by the college would be the dependent variable.

Although the main purpose of our experiment was to test this race and sex hypothesis, we were also interested in exploring the relationship between several additional variables and patterns of admission. Specifically, we were interested in differences between:

1) Large and small schools
2) Public and private institutions
3) Religious and secular schools
4) Small-town colleges and those in metropolitan areas
5) Southern institutions and those in other regions of the country
6) Junior colleges and four-year colleges

Procedure

A sample of 240 schools was randomly selected from *Lovejoy's College Guide.* (90) [See also Walster and Cleary, 157, and Walster et al., 156.] All schools in Wisconsin were excluded because a number of local admissions officers and administrators were used as consultants. Also excluded were colleges that required examinations other than the College Board tests or the American College Test (ACT). Some nursing schools, music colleges, and art institutes thus were eliminated.

In addition to race and sex, three levels of applicant ability were included to insure that our applicants would be neither accepted nor rejected by all colleges. The three levels of ability were used only as a safeguard: significance of the ability main effect was considered uninteresting because expected and because no interactions between ability and race or sex were predicted.

Thus a 2 x 2 x 3 design was used for this experiment: the sample of 240 colleges was divided randomly into 12 cells of 20 observations each.

Independent Variables

The race, sex, and ability levels of the candidates were randomly assigned, and one application was prepared for each of the sample colleges.

In order to generate the materials required for the college applications, we secured the school records of three real high school seniors with different ability levels and with names that did not reveal their sex. The manipulation of the two major independent variables, race and sex, was accomplished with the use of photographs which were attached to every application and also appeared on the Xeroxed copy of the transcript supposedly sent by the high school. The sex code was appropriately changed whenever it appeared.

The distinctions between the three ability levels were determined by students' actual records. The *Low Ability* candidate ranked 268 in a class of 414 and had a high school transcript on which this rank and appropriate course grades were recorded. He had an ACT composite score of 10 (09 in English, 18 in Mathematics, 07 in Social Science, and 06 in Natural Science). His College Board results were an SAT Verbal score of 404, an SAT Mathematics score of 382, and achievement scores of 451 in English, 442 in American History, and 356 in Mathematics.

The *Average Ability* candidate ranked 135 in a class of 414. He had an ACT composite score of 21 (19 in English, 16 in Mathematics, 26 in Social Science, and 22 in Natural Science). His College Board results were an SAT Verbal score of 504, an SAT score of 482 in Mathematics, and achievement scores of 531 in English, 522 in American History, and 436 in Mathematics.

The *High Ability* candidate ranked 55 in a class of 414. His ACT composite was 25 (23 in English, 22 in Mathematics, 29 in Social Science, and 27 in Natural Science). His College Board results were an SAT Verbal score of 604, an SAT Mathematics score of 582, and achievement scores of 591 in English, 582 in American History, and 526 in Mathematics.

To insure that applications would be as standard as possible, a master form was prepared. This form attempted to provide answers to any question that a college might ask. Included in this master application was basic information about the student's background, education, and interests. Also included were essays on his interests, hobbies, and religious experiences. Letters of reference, appropriate for students of any race or sex, were prepared. These recommendations were presumably from a minister, a teacher, a counselor, an employer, and a neighbor. The necessary medical records were prepared by a cooperating physician.

All applications were completed by referring to the master form. When the various documents were prepared, cooperating individuals signed and notarized them when necessary.

The personal interviews requested by some colleges posed an obvious problem. In most instances, however, we were able to plead inconvenience. Since we did not include Wisconsin colleges, most schools were relatively far from the applicant's home. In the one instance in which a personal interview had to be scheduled, the interviewer's cooperation was gained, and he based his evaluation on the information provided in the candidate's master application. In a second instance, an interviewer arrived unexpectedly at the high school. Fortunately, this interviewer was delighted to discover that his college had been chosen to participate in a research project. This school was considered as an "acceptance," since the admissions officer assured us that the high ability girl was definitely scheduled for acceptance.

The supplementary independent variables for post hoc analyses were obtained by letters to the colleges and from reference material. The letter, sent several months after the applications, asked the schools for the total day class enrollment and the number of males and females enrolled for either the spring semester 1967-68 or for fall of 1968-69. For the 16 schools which did not respond to the letter, the data were taken from the college catalog, *Lovejoy's College Guide*, (90) and the *College Blue Book* (25).

The same sources (i.e., college catalogs and *Lovejoy's*) were used to secure information on the type of school (i.e., religious or secular, public or private) and years of instruction offered. The urban population associated with the location of each school was obtained from 1960 census data.

We were especially interested in determining whether Southern schools differed in their pattern of admissions from schools in other regions of the country. We divided schools into four districts—Western, North Central, North Eastern, and Southern—on the basis of the U.S. Census classification. Schools located in Alabama, Arkansas, Delaware, Florida, Georgia, Kentucky, Louisiana, Maryland, Mississippi, North Carolina, Oklahoma, South Carolina, Tennessee, Texas, Virginia, and West Virginia were designated as "Southern" schools.

Dependent Variables

The main dependent variable was the acceptance or rejection of the candidate by the institution. The responses of the colleges were scored on a five-point scale:
1) Rejection
2) Rejection with the possibility of reconsideration at a later date
3) Qualified acceptance in which a program or course-work adjustment was stipulated
4) Acceptance
5) Acceptance with encouragement by a personal letter or an offer of unrequested financial aid.

In addition to this major dependent variable, three other measures were collected: the time between the candidate's initial request for application materials and the school's response; the nature of the reply; and the time between the mailing of the application and the school's decision. In the postcard sent to the school requesting application materials, the student indicated both his sex and race. A school, by neglecting to send the application forms, could delay or prevent a student's admission. Thus, the date on which the application request went out and the number of days it took before the school forwarded an application were tabulated. If the application form had not arrived by January 1, collaborators in other states secured application forms from the institution so that the school could be included in the experiment.

Most of the institutions responded simply by sending a catalog, application forms, and brochures of interest. But a personal cover letter expressing either encouragement or discouragement was sometimes included.

Results

Tables 1 and 2 contain the results of the analysis of variance on the main dependent variable, the measure of acceptance. Contrary to our expectation, neither the race nor the sex main effect was significant. (The F statistic testing the hypothesis that both main effects are null is 2.92, 2 and 228 d.f., $p < .06$.) Indeed, the race effect was not even in the predicted direction; blacks were accepted *less* frequently than were whites. (Even looking at the F statistic, which is a liberal test, $F = 2.30$, $p < .13$.) The data certainly provide no support for the notion that American colleges are actively recruiting Negro scholars. The sex effect was in the predicted direction. Males were preferred over females, but this difference was not significant ($F = 3.54$, $p < .06$).

TABLE 1

The Effect of Race, Sex, and Ability Level on an
Applicant's Chances of Admission to College

Applicant's			
Sex	Race	Ability Level	Admission Level[a]
Male	Black	Low	2.75
Male	Black	Medium	3.40
Male	Black	High	3.80
Male	White	Low	3.25
Male	White	Medium	3.55
Male	White	High	3.70
Female	Black	Low	1.85
Female	Black	Medium	3.20
Female	Black	High	4.05
Female	White	Low	2.00
Female	White	Medium	3.75
Female	White	High	4.05

[a] The higher the number, the greater the enthusiasm with which S was accepted for admission.

TABLE 2

Analysis of Variance for Admission Experiment

	df	F-Test	S-Test[a]	Critical Value
Main Effects				
A & B (Sex & Race)	2	2.92	....	3.04
A (Sex)	1	3.54	....	....
B (Race)	1	2.30	....	....
C_L (Linear Ability)	1	73.03	....	....
Interactions				
AB, AC, BC, & ABC	7	3.08[b]	....	2.05
AC_L (Sex x Linear Ability)	1	16.70	2.39[b]	2.05

[a] S-Test refers to the value of H. Scheffe's (130) statistic for the a posteriori analysis of a significant source of variation.

[b] $(P<.05)$.

A significant result that was not expected was found in the joint test of interactions. (See Figure 1 and Table 2.) At the low ability level males were preferred over females. At the higher ability level this

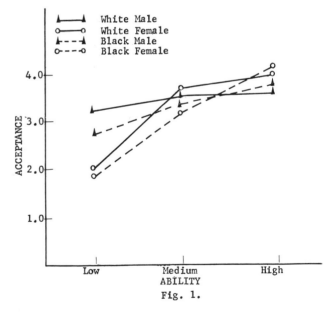

Fig. 1.

The effect of an applicant's sex, race, and ability level on his chance of college admission.

difference disappeared (S=2.39, p<.05). Since, in the actual high school populations, there are more students, both male and female, at the lowest of our ability levels than at the higher levels, it is clear that, *overall,* women are discriminated against in college admission.

The significant sex-by-ability interaction is in accord with the feminist observation (and complaint) that only a truly exceptional woman can ever hope to transcend sexual stereotypes and to be judged on an objective basis. A woman with more modest abilities continues to be judged as first and foremost a woman, and thus as an "inferior."

Analysis of Additional Variables

The reader will recall that we examined whether or not six dependent variables affected the pattern of our results. (These variables were: size of school, public/private school, religious/secular school, size of town in which school located, region of country in which school located, and junior college vs. four year college.) The evidence indicates that these factors did not alter the pattern of results secured. The supplementary dependent measures were essentially uncorrelated among themselves or with the acceptance measure. In addition, significant results were obtained with them no more frequently than would be expected by chance alone.

The failure to discover a different pattern of admissions in the South and the non-South was surprising to us. In view of historical differences between these regions, we had assumed that race and region might strongly interact in determining one's chances of admission. We speculated that while blacks might be actively recruited in non-Southern institutions, recruitment efforts would be much weaker in the South. The data indicate, however, that blacks are no more enthusiastically received in non-Southern institutions than they are in Southern ones. The race-region interaction is not significant (F=1.00, 1 and 216 d.f.), nor are the race-ability-region and the four-way interactions (F's=2.12 and 1.30 respectively).

IX

Coeducation

The force behind the coeducational movement is gaining momentum with every passing day—if recent statistics are to be accepted as a true reflection of the situation. During the past decade, the number of coeducational institutions in the United States rose from 1,533 to 2,226, according to the *Education Directory, Higher Education, 1970-71.* The number of institutions for men decreased from 236 to 154, while colleges and universities for women dropped from 259 to 193 during this same time period.

Separation of the sexes on academic as well as social levels appears to be weakening rapidly. Even the midwesterner, who has traditionally favored coeducation in the classroom but separation of the boys from the girls in the dorm, has begun to give in to the movement's strong persuasion. Recent figures from a Gallup Poll indicate that 46 percent of all parents interviewed would not mind if a daughter of theirs lived in a coeducational dormitory. Only 50 percent of the parents polled objected to coeducational living, with 4 percent undecided. Surveys conducted a number of months prior to this one had shown much greater opposition to coeducational living on our campuses.

In spite of the growing acceptance of the bringing together of the sexes, there are still many angry voices raised in opposition to the concept.

Richard E. Crockford, dean of faculty at Colby Junior College, says, "When the current romantic view of education as therapy has run its course, those two-year women's colleges which have remained true to their original purposes will be sought after by even more young women for the same reasons that motivated the founders of these institutions." (30)

Reprinted with permission from the *College Board Review*, No. 82 (Winter 1971-72) p. 17: College Entrance Examination Board, New York, December 1971.

D. M. Keezer says, "In my view . . . both the quality of women's education and the cultural influence of women in the United States will be downgraded if women's colleges mix up the sexes in a big way." (84)

"Until women are really equal," says Chatham College's president Edward D. Eddy, "there will be a need for a separate educational experience."

Obviously, the differences of opinion will not be easily resolved, nor will many of the problems in making the switch from unisex to coed. It's an unavoidable fact of life for some unisex schools in desperate fiscal difficulties that coeducation is a light at the end of the tunnel, and many schools have made, and will continue to make, the big switch rather than go under. Guidance counselors, teachers, administrators, admissions officers, and other educators are faced with a Pandora's Box when they approach the problem of coeducation.

X

How
Coeducation
Fails Women

Sheila Tobias

I want to talk to you about the state of coeducation, but instead of talking merely abstractly, I will tell you about Cornell University. It has an excellent reputation; it is partly state endowed and partly privately supported; and, at the time I worked there as Assistant to the Vice President for Academic Affairs, it certainly would have described itself as coed. Yet, Cornell was in so many ways inhospitable to women that I came to the conclusion that unless coeducation is accompanied by three features that I will describe—namely "liberated" counseling, a coeducational faculty, and women's studies—coeducation has to fail women.

Cornell was coeducational in law and to some extent in practice. But there was sex segregation by field. We had two undergraduate colleges, for example, that were respectively "male" and "female." The one was the College of Engineering which was 90 percent male and the other the then College of Home Economics which was something like 75 percent female. Part of the reason this last percentage was not even higher was that, in the year we were counting, the College of Home Economics was already trying to attract more male students and faculty as it redefined itself as the College of Human Ecology.

It is interesting that engineering, the male field, did not have the identity crisis that home economics, the female field, was undergoing. With the retirement of the Dean of Home Economics, a male dean was hired who was to guide the College into its new era. Whether this

Talk given at the University of Delaware, February 28, 1971. Printed with permission of the author.

development was right or wrong in terms of the nation's priorities is not at issue here. What is significant is that the process of modernization of a "female" science was done expressly at the expense of the ratio of women to men while the modernization of the College of Agriculture, for example, which has been going on since, has not involved an alteration in the predominantly male sex stereotypes or in the sex ratios of students or faculty.

The Colleges of Engineering and Veterinary Medicine did not discriminate against female applicants in a direct way. Rather, engineering did not go out of its way to encourage female high school students to consider engineering as a career, and veterinary medicine (at least until the year when the horse-loving daughter of one of the Cornell trustees got a negative reply to her letter of inquiry from the school) tended to discourage women applicants from entering the field altogether.

The imbalance of males and females in these latter schools could be explained away by the sex stereotyping of the culture, but the 3:2 male-female ratio in the College of Arts and Sciences at Cornell could not. We continually had an enormous number of women candidates who had to be refused admission into Arts because they were only allotted a 2:3 proportion of the openings. When this was challenged, we were shocked to hear the arguments in defense of the ratio: they ranged from the needs of the athletic teams to the "fact" that women are very poor alumni givers. (That they do not usually have control of large industrial monies was not mentioned.) A third reason was never said outright, but was always in the wings of the discussion: since women do not make a continuing contribution to society, it is really a waste of time to educate them, so we might as well educate as few of them as we have to. This last, interestingly enough, was less the view of the administrators who were more concerned about athletics and alumni giving; rather this was the view of segments of the male faculty. Of course, if we are going to use as a criterion for admission the anticipated contribution to society that the student will make, we will have to deal with some very difficult definitions.

The final argument which was said with a wink, a pinch, and a kind of giggle by the admissions committee (men giggle when they are feeling uncomfortable, just as women do) was of course that women prefer the 3:2 ratio because it increases the dating pool. We ignored this.

When we looked at the faculty ratios at Cornell we found that Engineering had a 100 percent male faculty and Home Economics about a 50 percent female faculty. More males were in those areas of Home Economics that had a future than in those that were being phased out. Of the 1400 faculty members then at Cornell (in 1969), 100 were women, and 75 of these were on the faculty of the College of Home Economics. This is why it is useful to do faculty ratios and faculty counts by school or department. Otherwise, a School of

Nursing or Home Economics can render misleading totals. Another thing to watch for is faculty category. Had we included lecturers and instructors not on the "academic ladder," we would have found more females teaching.

Most disturbing again was the College of Arts and Sciences. In the fields considered by counselors to be "feminine" (English, French, Art History, History, etc.) women were conspicuous by their absence on the faculty. History has never had a woman professor; neither had Government until 1971-72. In English there was not any woman on tenure then, and but one woman department chairman (Romance Languages) in the College.

Another area to investigate was the power positions of the faculty. This gives an index of the power wielded by groups: faculty committees, curriculum committees, elected faculty positions, etc. Again women were absent from these bodies. The only woman who was in a position of real power in the College of Arts and Sciences was the graduate field representative in the Department of Psychology. This woman was not a feminist; her function was to supervise the graduate activities of her department. Yet, in the two years or so that she was Field Representative, the percentage of females in the incoming graduate classes in Psychology approached 50 percent—the highest ratio in the College of Arts and Sciences. Today in her field, a clerk blocks out all references to the sex of the graduate applicant before it goes to faculty committee for evaluation.

There is an incredible amount of second guessing in faculty recommendations for female applicants to graduate school, we discovered. Reading some of these discreetly, we found phrases like "This woman is very unlikely to finish her degree because she is so pretty." And others like: "This woman is very unlikely to finish her degree. She is very insecure because she is not very pretty."

Fear of Success

For the past seven years, M. Horner has been studying what she calls achievement-related conflicts in women. (67) The nature of her research is to offer students a cue about a person and ask them to "fantasize"—tell a story—about that person. The cue she has used most is the sentence: "After first-term finals, John finds himself at the top of his medical school class." And the variation: "After first-term finals, Anne finds herself at the top of her medical school class."

The responses of normal, highly motivated students at the University of Michigan and at Wellesley College to these cues are: "John is a hard worker"; "he is getting what he deserves"; "this is how it should be"; "he expects to have a successful life"; etc. Some negative criticism of "John" reflects the new cynicism about material success and ambition altogether. But very few of the students tested reacted along the same range to Anne's success: 65 percent of the Michigan women, according to Horner, reflected a belief that Anne cannot be so successful without having conflicts with her "femininity." Anne is described as alone; she is pleased that she is first in her class but the price she has to pay is very high. Many of the answers are even more negative: Anne cheats; Anne's success is not really her own. Anne is ugly and has no choice but to succeed—that is, she has failed at man-catching. Still others are quite bizarre, hypothesizing that Anne does not really exist but is just the product of some male medical students' notion of what a female student would be like. Others tell of how Anne is punished by her fellow students for outdoing them.

In other studies, Horner gives groups of female and male students a TAT-type test and compares the stories they write by picture. For instance, she will show a group of women a picture of a male looking into a microscope. The women students generally agree that he represents competence; he is wearing a lab coat and looks like the professional he is. The stories these women write when given a picture of a *man* at work indicate that they do respect competence and professional success in general. But if the same group of women is shown (among many other pictures, of course) one of a woman in a lab coat looking into a microscope, they will respond negatively to that picture.

Horner's conclusions are that highly motivated and ambitious women suffer from ambivalent feelings about success; not that they want to fail—this would be masochism; rather, they have a high fear of the negative effects of success—high anxiety. If we find that our male professors are reinforcing, consciously or unconsciously, this fear of success, then we must reeducate the faculty about the results of research like Horner's and get them to change. This may mean hiring liberated males or males who feel differently about women or hiring women who feel very positively about women students.

Passivity and Dependence

One of the reasons a woman student has negative feelings about success is that she has never seen anybody who succeeded in the way she may wish to succeed. Some male professors put down their women colleagues. Our students are too bright not to notice the male faculty member's contempt for bright adult women. Such contempt is moreover reinforced by the faculty wife who has herself made the ultimate sacrifice of putting her husband's career ahead of her own. The students we interviewed at Cornell often made reference to the negative reinforcement they got from faculty wives.

In the classroom there is also some alienation which, although we have no statistically relevant documentation for it, women students feel. One bright woman complained that she felt inhibited in the classroom discussion section because it seemed to her that whenever she was very original or made an unexpected comment, she was treated as bizarre. She felt that the male students could "get away with" more original kinds of comments.

F. Howe has pointed out that women students have been rewarded in high school for being passive, dependent and avoiding conflict. (68) Meanwhile aggressiveness, active learning, and independence are rewarded in college, so they are constantly battling the old values against the new. Teachers do not expect aggressiveness from their women students. Indeed, when you do a good piece of work, chances are the professor will write on your paper: "You think like a man."

One of the problems graduate students have is that as the audience for their work becomes more generalized, they (the women students) have a harder time focusing on the adult approval which has motivated them in the past. Intellectual conflict is also difficult for the socialized female to cope with. Much of the time she avoids conflict, intellectual as well as interpersonal.

What happens in a coeducational school is, of course, that the style of teaching and the style of learning is that style that accommodates male students. We ask for, we expect, and we reward the kind of behavior that men find compatible with being male. That is, we create at the college level (not in the lower grades, by the way, for which our male children pay a high price [See Chapter III in this book]), an intellectual environment where aggressiveness, independence, and ability to cope with conflict are rewarded.

Inferiority

One of the important things that women are taught, in addition to the fact that they are different from men in our culture, is that they are inferior to men. This goes far to account for their reluctance to make their opinions known. It is not only that they do not want to be unpopular, that their date is in the classroom and he does not like aggressive women. That is part of it, but part of it also is that they do not believe that what they have to say is important.

At Connecticut College for Women some years ago, P. Goldberg did a study which has frequently been reported. (53) He handed out a series of essays to college women which included identical essays signed in one case by a male, in the second by a female. He asked the students to evaluate these, answering a series of questions, such as: What was the thesis? How was the thesis developed? What kind of evidence was brought to bear? Was it cogently argued? He found, over very large samples, that the essay would be undervalued when the author was allegedly a woman. Imagine what this kind of response does to the female teacher.

Other researchers later replicated this study in an even more interesting manner. Instead of asking the students to evaluate the essays (again identical, varying only in the authors' names), they asked the students direct factual questions based on the material they had read. They found that the students who had read the descriptive essay written allegedly by a woman tended to preface their remarks with "The author said . . ." and that the ones who had read essays putatively written by a man answered, "This is so." Apparently, then, there is a reluctance to accept what was written by a female to be a fact. The student who wrote "The author said . . ." was aiming to protect himself from any misstatement the author might have made. Even if the study has methodological faults, the conclusions are terrible. It tells us that students have trouble learning from us women; it tells us that no matter how many suits we file and how many women we force onto reluctant administrators, the students are not going to believe what they say or trust their minds to them.

Countering the implicit message that "female is inferior" is so massive a job, that it seems to me that we must counter the culture itself.

Countering the Culture

The first recommendation I would make toward countering the culture on the university campus is to "liberate" personal counseling from the *reality* emphasis (meaning that the student should always be encouraged to adapt to the situation, not the reverse). I think we must talk to our women students, and our men students, as if the situation in which they have grown up and the one they are living in now is not going to last forever. Our male students are revolting against male stereotypes. They are questioning the division of labor within the nuclear family, if not the nuclear family itself. So, in fairness to the students, our counselors should talk to them as if they are going to live very different, probably androgynous lives.

This means talking to women students as if they were going to have a life of their own, defined in terms of their abilities and potential, whether it is a career or a project or a political position. They should be encouraged to choose those subjects that will prepare them for this kind of life: hard, technological subjects, not just soft, liberal arts. The only women scientists we have working today are women who went to women's colleges where the male professor of physics or biology *had* to encourage women to enter his field if he was to have any students at all.

Liberated counseling also means facing the sexual facts. We are not dealing any longer with little girls whose mommies are expecting us to keep them from losing their virginity before they get out of college. We assume that our girls are probably going to get pregnant if we do not make contraception available to them.

The second area for action is in role modeling. We cannot force departments to go out and hire a female for every opening (as has been suggested at some universities). But we can force them to be candid about hiring females. We can demand money for special recruitment expenses such that a qualified woman can be brought in and apply for every opening. We must have this additional resource—it is the job I spend most time at on my campus—because otherwise what we call an "Old Boy" network operates at the recruitment level and it is one that excludes not only nonwhites but also females (see C. F. Epstein, 41). We must demand all openings be publicized so that persons not on the "Network" can inform others about openings.

The woman candidate has many disadvantages: her life style is different from her male colleagues. Much second guessing is done about her availability. At Cornell a woman who had received her Ph.D. some years before was mentioned as a candidate in Government. "She's married," several professors said, "and she won't want to leave her husband's area." It turned out she was no longer married and happy to leave, but the professors would not have consulted her about her plans had not a feminist been eavesdropping on their conversation and reacted.

Rarely is a competent woman really wooed by a university for a job. Several of the potential candidates whom I have invited to have a day of interviews have admitted to me at the end of the day that they did not do well at their interviews because they had never had the experience before. Yet, day-long interviews and colloquia are part of the academic ritual—one more experience women are locked out of. People who do these things all the time get fairly good at it. They are groomed for it.

Women's Studies

The third way of countering the culture is through women's studies. I think we could justify women's studies on many grounds: one of these is "equal time," since there have been glaring omissions in the curriculum. The history of women, for example, is never taught. There are dimensions in the psychology of sex differences that are not dwelled upon in psychology courses or in sociology courses. I like to say that the most appropriate way for a university to tackle the subject of sexism is *by studying it.*

In women's studies courses, we ask questions like the following: What does our society tell us about sex differences? What do other societies say about sex differences? What have we found out so far? What is the role of the media in perpetuating sex differences? We cannot change the culture overnight, but we can get a lot of people to stop and have a look at it.

The theme of the Cornell course was "The Evolution of Female Personality." We inquired: How much of female personality, as we know it, is innate and how much is learned? It was interdisciplinary; it had to be. We needed specialists in human development to tell us what they know about child development and sex-role socialization. What we learned from them is that video-taping *adult* behavior in infant wards reveals that male and female adults treat boy and girl babies differently. The boy is roughed up, touched, and handled more; the girl is talked to. We know, they say, that gender identity is established at 18 months. Little girls know that they are going to grow up to be mommies, even before they talk. Studies of children's literature reveal that in picture books there are no pictures of women driving cars. The closest adult women get to the outdoors is standing in the doorway. Little girls meanwhile are pictured watching and applauding the antics and achievements of little boys . . . just like mommy. [See Chapter IV in this book.]

Another part of the course is the study of the economic, social, and legal status of women in this country. Here we look at differential laws, differential wages and access to the trades, protective legislation, and the equal rights movement. The history of domestic life, the history of the family, the history of medicine, and of institution building on the local level, have all yet to be researched and written and this is of course the area in which women did play a role. But even there where women entered the male political scene as in the women's suffrage movement, there is silence, when not derision, in our history books.

One subject I added to this year's course that we did not touch on last year is the "masculine mystique." Last year we studied only the feminine mystique. We read Betty Friedan and had the students do a number of things such as content analyses of TV shows. We had them read six or more columns of marriage counseling as published regularly in the *Ladies' Home Journal,* and to pull out the assumptions underlying the "advice" about normal female behavior, about normal division of labor within marriage, etc.

We spend a fair amount of time on literature largely because, of the few women in proper faculty positions, the majority are in literature departments. But there are other more serious reasons to include literature. First, it is the only art form that women have been able to excel in, largely because it is the only art that does not require institutional support. To be a painter you need to be accepted by a school or by the master artist as his student; to be a playwright or to produce plays you need a whole, expensive organization. The only women who are well known in the theater arts are performing women for this reason (at least after men were no longer acceptable in the acting roles or singing roles of women). There is no doubt, as K. Millett has amply documented, that the most popular American twentieth century authors define women narrowly. (106)

The typical *Playboy* reader, by the magazine's own definition, is over 30 and earns $15,000, has at least a B.A., and has achieved management responsibility. Compare this to the "profile" of the *Playmate* who, is under 20, of lower class background, uneducated, paid about $70 per week (if she works at all), and (through a very devious mode of comparing her measurements with mine) *very short.* The ideal American female, then, is untalented, lower class, lower earning, short, and young; eminently manipulable, not likely to be smarter than a man, likely to be easily impressed.

Where we go from here in women's studies is still unknown, but, whether it will be a discipline on its own or an interdisciplinary study, it is absolutely imperative that undergraduates be exposed to this subject. We cannot allow women students in a coeducational atmosphere not to be given some support, some intellectual guidance, and some factual information to help them cope with the overwhelming experience of the college years in a coed institution: the experience of feeling inferior.

Without this compensation, coeducation will go on failing women.

XI

A Myth
Is Better
Than a Miss:
Men Get the Edge
in Academic Employment

Lawrence A. Simpson

In spite of the success of the melodic Virginia Slims television commercial, "You've come a long way, baby," recent events reveal that relatively few women have in fact come a long way in the area of employment. Ironically, discrepancies in male-female employment are prevalent in an area which is considered a liberator—education.

To determine if employing agents in higher education—deans, departmental chairmen, faculty—would express discriminatory employment attitudes toward academic women presented as being equally qualified with male competitors, and academic women presented as having superior qualifications to male competitors, I conducted a study in the spring of 1968 at six colleges in Pennsylvania. (138) An effort was also made to determine if employing agents would express a greater employment preference for male or female candidates presented for academic appointments. Finally, an additional goal of the study was to determine if employing agents in higher education who consistently reject female faculty candidates also place women in general in a subordinate position

Reprinted from *College & University Business,* February 1970. Copyrighted by McGraw-Hill, Inc.

The study was exploratory in nature and utilized a disguised structured attitude assessment technique designed to detect the expression of discriminatory attitudes toward professional academic women.

The research instrument was printed in booklet form and consisted of brief resume descriptions of fourteen individuals presented as candidates for hypothetical higher education positions. The resumes were presented in seven pairs, with a male and female candidate in each pair except the first, where two males were presented in an effort to prevent the subjects from developing an immediate reaction to the intentional sex nature of the instrument.

Utilizing a semi-simulation approach that presented a modified forced-choice format, the subjects were requested to assume that a vacancy existed in their department at a particular academic level. Additionally, they were to assume that their single employment choice was to be made from the two candidates presented in each pair.

Four of the resume pairs presented males and females judged to have equal qualifications; two resume pairs presented females with superior qualifications to the males in each case. Full-face photographs accompanied all resumes which contained background data equal in all relevant respects except sex. In an effort to ensure the equal nature of the instrument, two forms were developed by reversing the photographs and names of the candidates and holding constant the descriptive material.

An employment preference rating scale followed each resume. The five-point scale provided a range from strongly preferable to strongly unpreferable. Space was provided which allowed the subjects an opportunity to indicate their rationale for appointing or not appointing each candidate. Provisions were also made to allow the subjects to indicate in brief sentences comments relative to their rationale for appointing or not appointing each candidate presented in the resume instrument.

The final portion of the instrument presented a 12 item adaptation of the Open Subordination of Women Attitude Scale. In order to disguise the blunt nature of this scale, the items were intermingled with 24 unrelated attitude statements. Only the 12 Open Subordination of Women Attitude Scale items were analyzed. The purpose of this scale was to determine if employing agents who reject academic women for employment also place women in general in a subordinate position.

The subjects consisted of deans, departmental chairmen, and total faculty in selected academic fields at six Pennsylvania institutions of higher education. The academic areas included French-Spanish, English, and art as high female employment fields and political science, philosophy, and history as fields employing a significantly lower percentage of women than the 18 percent average for all fields.

The institutions included two public state colleges, one private women's college, one private men's university, and two public universities.

A total of 369 instruments were distributed and resulted in a return of 257 of which 234 were usable.

A major outcome of the study was the demonstration that discriminatory attitudes toward academic women were exhibited by the sampled employing agents when considering equally qualified male and female candidates. When all variables were equal except sex, the male candidate was typically chosen for employment. This finding is consistent with findings in an unpublished doctoral thesis prepared by H. Berwald, which indicated that deans, department chairmen, and faculty do not feel that employment opportunities are equal for men and women and that hiring officials' employment attitudes and practices strongly favor the selection of males to the faculty. (15)

On the other hand, employing agents selected for employment a statistically significant number of superior females in preference to less qualified males. This finding is consistent with previous research which suggested that hiring officials tend to employ highly qualified females if qualified males are not available.

It was found that there were no significant differences between the employing agent levels of deans, departmental chairmen, and faculty in their discriminatory employment attitudes toward female candidates who were judged to be equally qualified with male candidates. Correspondingly, there were no significant differences between the employing agent levels in their consistent selection of superior females. These findings are contradictory to Berwald's research, which indicated that departmental chairmen typically displayed a higher degree of preference for male faculty. It would appear that less superior academic women may face employment roadblocks at all employing agent levels.

The study also attempted to determine if significant differences in the employment of academic women would be observed between academic fields which demonstrate relatively high and low percentages of female faculty. It was determined that the high female employment fields group selected significantly more equally qualified females than did the low female employment fields group. Superior females, like the equal females, experienced statistically significant discriminatory employment attitudes from the low female employment fields group. No clues were observed to account for this outcome.

When study participants were requested to express a rating of employment preference for the male and female candidates presented, statistically significant differences were found between the ratings for equal male and female candidates. The subjects expressed a higher degree of preference for the equal male candidates than for the equal female candidates. Conversely, superior female candidates were rated significantly higher than the less qualified male candidates.

Age, sex, and experience of the subjects were found to have a significant influence on the employment selection of female candidates while degree and rank did not exert a significant influence on the employment selection of female candidates. Subjects in the 20 to 30 age range and subjects over 60 years of age selected the highest number of female candidates. Subjects in the 41 to 50 age bracket selected the least number of female candidates. In terms of years of experience, the subjects with less than five years of experience and subjects with over 20 years of experience chose the highest number of female candidates. Subjects with 16 to 20 years of experience chose the least number of females. As might be expected, female subjects selected substantially more female candidates than did males.

The final major goal of the study was to determine if the higher education employing agents sampled who consistently rejected female faculty candidates would also place women in general in a subordinate position. Correlations revealed that subjects who tended to select for employment a high number of female faculty candidates did express positive attitudes toward women in general as measured by the Open Subordination of Women Attitude Scale. Subjects who selected a low number of female candidates typically expressed negative attitudes toward women.

It should be clear that the findings of this study are derived from a restricted population and generalizations should be made with this fact in mind. However, prospective academic women must be realistically aware of the employment limitations that may prevail. Women should recognize, well in advance of their venture into the academic marketplace, that they typically may not be selected on an equal basis with males. Prospective academic women must recognize that they should, in effect, be more highly qualified than their male competitors for higher education positions. Additionally, women should be aware of the attitudes that may be expected from employing agents in the academic fields which typically employ few females.

Perhaps the most important implication of the study is that employing agents in higher education must seriously re-examine their own attitudes regarding academic women and be keenly aware of any prejudices or rationalizations which cause academic women to be treated in any way other than as productive human beings. In a period when higher education faces an acute shortage of qualified teachers, the denial of a teaching position to a qualified female applicant, based solely on the negative attitudes toward women of an employing agent, is open to serious question.

XII

Women
in Universities

Ethel Bent Walsh

Historically, institutions of higher learning have been regarded as the standard bearers of high moral, ethical, and democratic conduct. Historically, members of their faculties have awakened the social conscience of continents and encouraged the assult against those who would stifle the mental, physical, or emotional progress of mankind. Historically, national, regional, and local governments have sought the intellectual assistance of faculty members in solving social problems. Is it possible, then, that there can be sexual bias in academe, that bastion of tolerance and reasonableness? The answer is affirmative as evidenced by statistical data: the many statements made at the *Hearings on Section 805 of H. R. 10698 before the Special Subcommittee on Education of the House Committee on Education and Labor,* 91st Congress, 2nd Session (1970)*; the filing of charges of sex discrimination against 350 colleges and universities by the Women's Equity Action League (WEAL) and the National Organization for Women (NOW); recent court decisions; as well as current and pending legislation.

I would like to express appreciation to Ms. Sonia Pressman Fuentes and Ms. Elsa Glass of the Office of General Counsel, the Equal Employment Opportunity Commission, for their assistance in preparing this presentation, "The Role of Government in the Attainment of Equal Opportunity for Women in Universities," a paper presented at the American Association for the Advancement of Science, Philadelphia, Dec. 1971. (E.B.W.)

*All quotations from these *Hearings* will be identified in the text by (*Hearings* 1970).

Discrimination in Admissions

There exists in our colleges and universities today what Bernice Sandler has described as "a massive, consistent and vicious pattern of sex discrimination" (*Hearings* 1970). This pattern is accomplished by (a) admission quotas in undergraduate and graduate schools; (b) higher admission standards for women than for men; (c) and discrimination in financial assistance for graduate study (scholarships, fellowships, research grants, teaching assistantships, etc.).

Peter Muirhead, Associate Commissioner of Education, showed that at Cornell University, there were quotas on women applicants at all the schools in the institution. For example:

. . . in the State School of Agriculture quotas exist such that the Mean SAT (Scholastic Aptitude Test) scores of entering women freshmen are higher than those of men by 30-40 points. (*Hearings* 1970) [See also Chapter X in this book.]

Muirhead further stated that restrictive admission policies were applicable at public universities as well as private institutions:

We know that many colleges admit fixed percentages of men and women each year, resulting in a freshman class with fewer women meeting higher standards than it would contain if women were admitted on the same basis as men. At Cornell University for example, the ratio of men to women remains 3 to 1 from year to year; at Harvard-Radcliffe, it is 4 to 1. The University of North Carolina at Chapel Hill's Fall 1969 "Profile of the Freshman Class" states that admission of women on the freshman level will be restricted to those who are especially well qualified. They admitted 3,231 men, or half of the male applicants, and 747 women, about one-fourth of the female applicants. Chapel Hill is a state-supported institution. (*Hearings* 1970)

Another state-supported school, the University of Virginia at Charlottesville, had a "male only" admission policy. Several women plaintiffs sued in the U.S. District Court alleging that they had been denied their constitutional rights of equal protection of the law as guaranteed by the Fourteenth Amendment.* The Federal Court held that the exclusion of women applicants from the all-male campus of the University of Virginia was a denial of equal protection where the facilities available to women were not equal.

A more consistent use of discriminatory quotas in graduate schools is revealed by Ann Sutherland Harris of Columbia University, who stated it was easier for a man than a woman to get into graduate school:

The most conclusive evidence is the grade point average of the women which is significantly higher than the men. 9.1 percent of the women reported straight A averages compared with 6.8 percent of the men; 24.9 percent of the women reported A- averages compared to 20.1 percent of the men; and 32.2

Kirstein v. *Rectors and Visitors of the University,* 309 F. Supp. 184 E.D.Va., 1970.

percent of the women had B+ averages compared with 31.6 percent of the men. Only 30 percent of the women but 41 percent of the men had a grade average of B or lower. (*Hearings* 1970; 65)

In the professional schools, the discrimination in admissions becomes more acute. Frances S. Norris testified that while women applicants to medical schools have increased over 300 percent since 1930, the proportion of women accepted has fallen. From 1930 to 1969, women's share of the total number of admissions rose from 4.5 percent to 9.7 percent, but the percentage of women applicants accepted over this same period decreased from 65.5 percent to 46.5 percent. Norris reiterated that the low percentage of women accepted to medical schools results from admitted prejudice of the admissions committees:

Interview with admission officers at 25 Northeastern Medical Schools revealed that 19 admitted they accepted men in preference to women unless the women were demonstrably superior. (*Hearings* 1970)

Similarly, law schools have unwritten quota systems for female applicants. Female applicants are scrutinized for ability and motivation and even their marital status is questioned before granting admission because, as one admissions officer stated, "a female student might not graduate and continue to practice."(38) It would follow that a male applicant is often chosen over an equally qualified female.

Strong-voiced complaints have been lodged against the financial assistance policies of universities especially with respect to research and graduate study programs. In 1969, women represented 33 percent of the graduate student population; they received 28 percent of the awards given under NDEA Title IV fellowship programs for graduate students and 29.3 percent of the graduate academic awards under NDEA Title VI. Direct evidence of discrimination in the award of scholarships and fellowships was presented against New York University and Cornell:

N.Y.U. has totally excluded women for more than 20 years from the prestigious and lucrative Root-Tilden and Snow Scholarships. Twenty Root-Tilden Scholarships worth more than $10,000 each were awarded to male future public leaders each year. Women, of course, can't be leaders and N.Y.U. contributed its share to making that presumption a reality by its exclusionary policy. (Diane Blank and Susan D. Ross, *Hearings* 1970)

A similar charge against Cornell University stated that the Cornell catalogue lists scholarships and prizes open to arts and science undergraduates totaling $5,045 annually to be distributed on the basis of sex. Women are eligible to receive only 15 percent or $760.00 of this amount compared with $4,285.00 for men. (Ella Kusnetz and Barbara Frances, *Hearings* 1970)

Undergraduate and graduate programs in universities are analogous to the training and apprenticeship programs of industry,

Congresswoman Martha Griffiths (D-Mich.) has pointed out.* The relationship between training and employment is an integral one. Accordingly, discrimination in the admission of women to undergraduate and graduate schools, and sex discrimination in the grant of scholarships, seriously detracts from the ability of women to compete in the labor market.

Discrimination in Employment

Discrimination in the employment of women as teachers and administrative personnel begins with elementary school and becomes geometrically worse through the college and professional school levels. (126) While 67.6 percent of the elementary and secondary school teachers are women, only 22 percent of the elementary school principals and only 4 percent of the secondary school principals are women. Furthermore, of the 13,000 school superintendents, only two are women.

The higher the rank, the fewer the women. For example, the last time a woman was hired as a professor in the Department of Psychology at the University of California in Berkeley was in 1924. (112) Yet, women received 23 percent of the doctorates in psychology at this University. At Columbia University, there is no woman on the faculty of the Department of Psychology although 36 percent of the doctorates in that field are awarded to women. (Sandler, *Hearings* 1970) At the University of Chicago, the percentage of women faculty members is less now than it was in 1899.

A 1966 survey conducted by the National Education Association found that in a nationwide study of degree-granting institutions, including junior colleges, women represented 18.4 percent of the full-time faculty. (Muirhead, *Hearings* 1970) Of this 18.4 percent, 32.5 percent were instructors; 19.4 percent were assistant professors; 15.1 percent were associate professors; and 8 percent were full professors. An even darker picture emerges from the realization that women comprise less than 10 percent of the total faculty in the prestigious private institutions and large state universities. A report on the distribution of women faculty members at ten high endowment institutions in 1960 showed women ranged from 9.8 percent of the instructors to 2.6 percent of the full professors. (117) In a survey of ten high enrollment institutions, women faculty members comprised 20.4 percent of the instructors; 12.7 percent of the assistant professors; 10.1 percent of the associate professors; and 4.3 percent of the full professors.**

---

*116 *Cong. Rec.*, H. 1588, March 9, 1970.

**The ten high endowment colleges were: Chicago, Columbia, Cornell, Harvard, Johns Hopkins, M.I.T., Northwestern, Princeton, Stanford, and Yale. Eight institutions reported. The ten high enrollment institutions were: Berkeley, C.C.N.Y., Indiana, Illinois, Michigan, Michigan State, Minnesota, N.Y.U., Ohio State, and Pennsylvania State.

A. S. Rossi conducted a study in 188 graduate departments in sociology in 1968-1969.(127)   Women were 30 percent of the Ph.D. candidates, 27 percent of the full-time instructors, 14 percent of the full-time assistant professors, 9 percent of the full-time associate professors, 4 percent of the full-time professors, 1 percent of the chairmen of graduate sociology departments, and 0 percent of the 44 full professors in the five elite institutions: Berkeley, Chicago, Columbia, Harvard, and Michigan.

In 1968-69, when women constituted 22 percent of the graduate students and were awarded 19 percent of the Ph.D.'s at the Harvard University Graduate School of Arts and Sciences, there was not one woman among the more than 400 tenured professors in that graduate school. (Sandler, *Hearings* 1970) Simpson discovered in his study of hiring agents that, where men and women were equally qualified, hiring officials favored the selection of males for faculty appointments, even in all-female institutions. [See Chapter XI in this book.] As a result, prospective academic women must recognize that they must be more highly qualified than their male counterparts for positions in higher education.

The effect of rules against nepotism, which bar two members of a family from teaching at the same university, falls predominately on academic women married to academic men. A report at the University of California at Berkeley included a survey of 23 women with Ph.D.'s who were married to men teaching at the University. The survey found that while these women were qualified for full-time work, they held temporary or part-time positions and their talents, accordingly, were not fully utilized.(18)   Ann Scott of the University of Buffalo has stated that the "no-inbred-hiring" rule, whereby a department or university refuses to hire any person who holds a degree from that university, prevents women who marry faculty men and work for a degree at their husband's university from securing a position at that university after graduation. (*Hearings* 1970)

Scott further contends that the tenure system is "one of the most powerful and unexamined areas of discrimination against women in the university world." She suggests that in the matter of tenure the university

can effect some reforms to bleed the system of sexist bias. It can adopt a broader base of tenure criteria to include emphasis upon teaching, service to the University and the community and the necessity of women as visible life models. Because tenure means promotion, and because the patterns clearly show that as presently practiced it discriminates against women as a *selection system,* the whole tenure procedure should be subjected to a validation study on this basis alone. (*Hearings* 1970)

Secret proceedings in which a candidate's future career is decided *ex parte* could tend to discriminate against women.

Blanket mandatory maternity leave provisions also cause teachers at all levels to lose their tenure and seniority rights. Maternity leave policies in educational institutions requiring teachers to leave after the fourth or fifth month of pregnancy have been attacked in the courts as violations of the Fifth and Fourteenth Amendments. There have only been two court decisions in this area to date, and they reached contradictory conclusions. In *LaFleur* v. *Cleveland Board of Education* it was held that the maternity leave policy of the Board of Education was not a denial of equal protection of the law under the Fourteenth Amendment. However, the Court in *Cohen* v. *Chesterfield County School Board,* a Virginia case, ordered the restoration of tenure to an elementary school teacher who was subject to a similar maternity leave policy. There, the Court held that the policy of the Board of Education did deny females equal protection of the laws. A complaint has recently been filed in Alabama by five black teachers who were dismissed or forced to resign, losing their tenure rights, because of the maternity policy of the Phenix City Board of Education.*

In the case of *Hill* v. *Chartiers Valley Joint School District,* Mrs. Hill, an elementary school teacher in Thornburg, Pennsylvania, was dismissed by her school board after she gave birth to a child while on sabbatical leave. She brought suit on the ground that her dismissal had not been in accordance with the procedural requirements set forth in the School Code Act of 1911, and won reinstatement to her job with back pay.**

The Role of Government

In view of the fact that teachers in colleges and universities, as well as schools in general, are currently exempt from Federal legislation and regulation, except for Executive Order 11246, they have frequently resorted to the Constitution for relief, as is evidenced by the cases attacking the maternity leave policies of school systems. (Relief would be sought under the Fifth and Fourteenth Amendments to the Constitution and under 42 U.S.C. Secs. 1981 and 1983.) Such relief is, however, available only where the school involved is an instrumentality of the municipal, state, or local government.

Executive Order 11246, as amended by 11375, effective October 1968, prohibits discrimination based on race, color, religion, sex, and national origin by contractors and subcontractors of the Federal Government (with contracts of $10,000 or more) and on federally assisted construction contracts. The Order is administered by the Office of Federal Contract Compliance (the OFCC) in the Department of Labor.

---

*LaFleur v. *Cleveland Board of Education,* 326 F. Supp. 1159 (E.D. Va., 1971), appeal pending No. 71-1707 (4th Cir.); *Cohen* v. *Chesterfield County School Board,* 236 F. Supp. 1159 (E.D. Va., 1971) appeal pending No. 71-1707 (4th Cir.); *Ford* v. *Brown* (N.D. Ala., 1971).

**Chartiers Valley Joint School Board v. *Hill,* Case No. 3051 (Sup. Ct. of Pa., 1968).

There is no doubt that the Congress of the United States and the Executive Branch of our Government are determined to adopt and enforce measures that will effectively end discrimination in the public sector, the private sector, and the educational sector. Let us not dwell on past failures and sins of omission that have made this role of government necessary. We are all well aware of the extraordinary social, political, economic, and cultural change that has characterized the past several years. Essentially, it is a revolution in values which has resulted in a reexamination of the value system upon which our country was founded and with which it prospered mightily—but a value system which unfortunately perpetuates inequities in the opportunities open to some in our society. Let us rather concentrate our efforts on anticipating areas of social concern and developing and inaugurating effective programs to meet these needs. Only by so doing can academe preserve a larger measure of its traditional independence, while at the same time responding to the clear demands of the American people. The academic community can no longer afford to neglect any of those who are a part of it, for the integrity of the whole depends upon the strength of its parts.

XIII

Comment:
"Education's
and Not Nature's Fools"*

Scarvia B. Anderson

There *are* sex differences—physiological, psychological, and social. Some are obvious to the casual observer; others have been well documented in the annals of social science and medical research. Although many people still see much to be desired in personal and institutional attitudes toward the sexes, there is little argument today that such differences should be interpreted in "deficit" terms or that they automatically imply discrimination. There is little argument either with the fact that within-sex differences are almost always greater than "average" differences between the sexes. There are many arguments about whether sex differences are innate, culturally induced, or—likely in the majority of cases—the product of interactions between genetic and environmental variables. These arguments are not dangerous but rather are valuable as long as they remain in the scientific arena of theories, hypotheses, and proofs.

Educators can almost escape the whole problem: they **are** enlightened enough not to interpret sex differences as deficiencies (in either sex); they know there are wide individual differences within the sexes; they are not expected by training or role definition to be any more than interested spectators in the arena of scientific inquiry into the causes of sex differences; they can always blame the home or society for the stereotypes and stigmas associated with the accident of being born a boy or a girl; they can even say that the school is just a reflection of the culture and rest relatively secure in the philosophy that "education should be accommodated to the state of society, manners, and government of the country in which it is

---

*Lady Winchelsea's early eighteenth century protest about women. (122)

conducted."(128)   *Except* that the state of society, manners, and government of this country is changing very rapidly. (In many other contexts, our public and private schools and colleges have been characterized as anachronistic—see references 4; 74; 121; 137.) *Except* that for educators to continue to blame the home and society for what schools do or do not do rather than to be accountable for the twelve, thirteen, sixteen, or more years of priority contact they have with willing and unwilling students is a cop out.

We have shown with a very limited sampling of data and opinion that downright sex discrimination or subtle sex bias pervades all of American education from nursery through graduate school. The consequences for a boy who decides to be a kindergarten teacher or a girl who decides to be a physicist are severe. Even greater consequences are suffered by the boy who was never allowed to consider kindergarten teaching as a career, who had to hide poetry books in his locker, and who did not find out until he was forty that indoor cooking—or a conversation with a woman lawyer—could be fun; or by the girl who was told that it was O.K. for her to flunk algebra tests because girls were not expected to "do math," who was ostracized by her friends because she excelled at baseball, and who was discouraged from entering graduate school because she was "too pretty"—and was left with two children to support when her husband was run over by a bulldozer.

It is hoped that this book will add its small weight to the pressures for "consciousness raising," that phenomenon which members of the women's liberation movement put so much stock in. It asks educators, first, to be sensitive to the differences—sex-associated *or not*—they find among the boys, girls, men, and women they consider, select, admit, administer, teach, and counsel. All of these differences are to be respected; some are to be cherished and, if possible, enhanced. The world may have even more need for Thomas Jeffersons, Margaret Sangers, Duke Ellingtons, Maria Montessoris, and Louis Pasteurs in the future than it had in the past. Certainly it will not be able to afford large numbers of citizens who have been denied the opportunity to develop their own identities and individual bases of behavior—whether through malice or default or in the name of "democratic" education.

Awareness of individual differences will, of course, point to some needs for improvement or remediation; not to attempt to correct a defect, teach a skill, or illuminate an attitude important to an individual's personal or social development is as irresponsible as a lock-step approach. It is especially in this area that educators will note some differences that seem to have arisen from arbitrary or capricious treatments of certain sexes, classes, races, or other groups of people. And it will surely occur to them to scrutinize the treatments they apply and the decisions they make for instances of discrimination, bias, or stereotyping that have little to do with the individual case.

Gloria Steinem has said that "If women's lib wins, perhaps we all do." (143) Certainly if educators will stop and examine their attitudes toward male and female students and colleagues, analyze what they consciously or unconsciously do to them, see some of the irony as well as the social significance in the situation, and start taking seriously their own mottoes about "child-centered experiences" and "individual development," the battle will be almost over.

References

(1) Allen, S. A.; Spear, P. S.; and Lucke, J. R. "Effects of Social Reinforcement on Learning and Retention in Children." *Developmental Psychology* 5 (1971): 73-80.

(2) Anastasi, A. *Differential Psychology: Individual and Group Differences in Behavior* (3rd ed.). New York: Macmillan, 1958.

(3) Anastasiow, N. J. "Success in School and Boys' Sex-Role Patterns." *Child Development* 36 (1965): 1053-1066.

(4) Anderson, S. B. "Accountability: What, Who and Whither?" *School Management* 15, No. 9 (1971): 28-29, 50.

(5) Angoff, W. H. (ed.) *The College Board Admissions Testing Program: A Technical Report on Research and Development Activities Relating to the Scholastic Aptitude Test and Achievement Tests.* New York: College Entrance Examination Board, 1971.

(6) Astin, H. S. *The Woman Doctorate in America.* New York: Russell Sage Foundation, 1969.

(7) Barron, F. "Originality in Relation to Personality and Intellect." *Journal of Personality* 25 (1957): 730-742.

(8) Bayley, N. "Individual Patterns of Development." *Child Development* 27 (1956): 45-74.

(9) Bayley, N. "Data on the Growth of Intelligence Between 16 and 21 Years as Measured by the Wechsler-Bellevue Scale." *Journal of Genetic Psychology* 90 (1957): 3-15.

(10) Bayley, N., and Oden, M. H. "The Maintenance of Intellectual Ability in Gifted Adults." *Journal of Gerontology* 10 (1955): 91-107.

(11) Bayley, N., and Schaefer, E. S. "Correlations of Maternal and Child Behaviors With the Development of Mental Abilities: Data from the Berkeley Growth Study." *Monographs of the Society for Research in Child Development* 29, No. 6 (1964): 3-79.

(12) Beller, E. K. "A Study of Dependency and Aggression in Early Childhood." Progress Report, Project M-849, Child Development Center, New York, N. Y., 1962.

(13) Bentzen, F. "Sex Ratios in Learning and Behavior Disorders." *The National Elementary Principal* 46 (1966): 13-17.

(14) Berry, J. L., and Martin, B. "GSR Reactivity as a Function of Anxiety, Instructions and Sex." *Journal of Abnormal and Social Psychology* 54 (1957): 9-12.

(15) Berwald, H. "Attitudes Toward Women College Teachers in Institutions of Higher Education Accredited by the North Central Association." Unpublished dissertation, University of Minnesota, 1962.

(16) Bradway, K. P., and Thompson, C. W. "Intelligence at Adulthood: A 25-Year Follow-up." *Journal of Educational Psychology* 53 (1962): 1-14.

(17) Brim, O. G. "Family Structure and Sex Role Learning by Children: A Further Analysis of Helen Kock's Data." *Sociometry* 21 (1958): 1-16.

(18) California, University of, Berkeley. Report of the Subcommittee on the Status of Academic Women on the Berkeley Campus, May 1970.

(19) Carey, G. L. "Reduction of Sex Differences in Problem Solving by Improvement of Attitude through Group Discussion." Unpublished doctoral dissertation, Stanford University, 1955.

(20) Carlsmith, L. "Effect of Early Father Absence on Scholastic Aptitude." *Harvard Educational Review* 34 (1964): 3-21.

(21) Carlson, R. O. "Variation and Myth in the Social Status of Teachers." *Journal of Educational Sociology* 35 (1961): 104-118.

(22) Carter, R. S. "How Invalid Are Marks Assigned by Teachers?" *Journal of Educational Psychology* 43 (1952): 218-228.

(23) Coffman, W. E. "Sex Differences in Responses to Items in an Aptitude Test." *18th Yearbook, National Council on Measurement in Education* (1961): 117-124.

(24) Coleman, J. S. *The Adolescent Society.* Glencoe, Ill.: Free Press, 1961.

(25) *College Blue Book.* New York: CCM Corporation, 1967.

(26) Colombotos, J. L. "Sex Role and Professionalism: A Study of High School Teachers." *The School Review* 71 (1963): 27-40.

(27) Corwin, R. G. *Militant Professionalism*. New York: Appleton-Century-Crofts, 1970.

(28) Crandall, V. C. "Sex Differences in Expectancy of Intellectual and Academic Reinforcement." In C. P. Smith (ed.), *Achievement-Related Motives in Children*. New York: Russell Sage Foundation, 1969, pp. 11-45.

(29) Crandall, V. J.; Katkovsky, W.; and Preston, A. "Motivational and Ability Determinants of Young Children's Intellectual Achievement Behaviors." *Child Development*, 1962, 33, 643-661.

(30) Crockford, R. E. "The Forgotten Sex in Education." *Junior College Journal* 42, No. 2 (1971): 17-19.

(31) Cross, K. P. *The Undergraduate Woman*. Research Report No. 5. Washington, D.C.: American Association for Higher Education, 1971.

(32) D'Andrade, R. G. "Sex Differences and Cultural Institutions." In E. E. Maccoby (ed.), *The Development of Sex Differences*. Stanford, Calif.: Stanford University Press, 1966, pp. 173-204.

(33) Davidson, H. H., and Lang, G. "Children's Perceptions of Their Teachers' Feelings Toward Them Related to Self-perception, School Achievement, and Behavior." *Journal of Experimental Education* 29 (1960): 107-118.

(34) Davidson, K. S., and Sarason, S. B. "Test Anxiety and Classroom Observations." *Child Development* 32 (1961): 199-210.

(35) Davis, H.; Ware, M. L.; Shapiro, F. S.; Donald, E.; and Stieber, G. N. "Economic, Legal and Social Status of Teachers." *Review of Educational Research* 33 (1963): 398-414.

(36) Davis, O., and Slobodian, J. "Teacher Behavior Toward Girls and Boys During First Grade Reading Instruction." *American Educational Research Journal* 4 (1967): 261-269.

(37) DeCrow, K. "You've Got To Be Carefully Taught." Paper presented at the Susan B. Anthony Conference on Women, Syracuse, February 1970.

(38) Dinerman, B. "Sex Discrimination In the Legal Profession." *American Bar Association Journal* 55 (1969): 951-954.

(39) Dreeben, R. *The Nature of Teaching*. Glenview, Ill.: Scott, Foresman, 1970.

(40) Ebert, E., and Simmons, K. "The Brush Foundation Study of Child Growth and Development. I: Psychometric Tests." *Monographs of the Society for Research in Child Development* 8, No. 2 (1943).

(41) Epstein, C. F. "Encountering the Male Establishment: Sex-Status Limits on Women's Careers in the Professions." *American Journal of Sociology* 75 (1970): 965-982.

(42) Erikson, E. H. "Inner and Outer Space: Reflections on Womanhood." *Daedalus* 93 (1964): 582-606.

(43) Fagot, B. I., and Patterson, G. R. "An In Vivo Analysis of Reinforcing Contingencies for Sex-Role Behaviors in the Preschool Child." *Developmental Psychology* 1 (1969): 563-568.

(44) *Financial Status of the Public Schools, 1969*. Washington, D.C.: National Education Association, Committee on Education Finance, 1969.

(45) Fisher, E. "The Second Sex, Junior Division." *The New York Times Book Review*, May 24, 1970, 6-7. ©1970 by the New York Times Company. Reprinted by permission.

(46) Folger, J. K., and Nam, C. B. *Education of the American Population* (1960 Census Monograph). Washington, D.C.: U.S. Government Printing Office, 1967.

(47) Freeman, J. "Dissent" [to University of Chicago report]. *School Review* 79 (1970): 115-118.

(48) French, J. W. "A Study of Emotional States Aroused During Examinations." College Entrance Examination Board, Research and Development Reports, and ETS Research Bulletin 61-6, Princeton, N. J.: Educational Testing Service, 1961.

(49) Friedman, P., and Bowers, N. "Student Imitation of a Rewarding Teacher's Verbal Style as a Function of Sex and Grade Level." *Journal of Educational Psychology* 62 (1971): 487-491.

(50) Gaier, E. L., and Collier, M. J. "The Latency-Stage Story Preference of American and Finnish Children." *Child Development* 31 (1960): 431-451.

(51) Gates, A. "Sex Differences in Reading Ability." *Elementary School Journal* 61 (1961): 431-434.

(52) Gittell, M. "Teacher Power and Its Implications for Urban Education." *Theory into Practice* (April 1968): 80-82.

(53) Goldberg, P. "Are Women Prejudiced Against Women?" *Transaction* (April 1968): 28-30.

(54) Goldberg, S., and Lewis, M. "Play Behavior in the Year-Old Infant: Early Sex Differences." *Child Development* 40 (1969): 21-31.

(55) Goldman, R. *Exploring Our Needs.* Chicago: Follett, 1967.

(56) Good, T. L., and Brophy, J. E. "Do Boys and Girls Receive Equal Opportunity in First Grade Reading Instruction?" (Report series No. 24.) Research and Development Center for Teacher Education, University of Texas, Austin, 1969.

(57) Goodwin, H. I., and Carlton, P. (eds.) *Above the Salt: Militancy in Education.* Morgantown, W. V.: West Virginia University, College of Human Resources and Education, 1968.

(58) Groff, P. J. "The Social Status of Teachers." *Journal of Educational Sociology* 36 (1962): 20-25.

(59) Gross, E. "Plus ca Change? Sexual Structure of Occupations Over Time." *Social Problems* (Fall 1968): 198-208.

(60) Guilford, J. P. "The Structure of Intellect." *Psychological Bulletin* 53 (1956): 267-293.

(61) Haan, N. "Proposed Model of Ego Functioning: Coping and Defense Mechanisms in Relationship to I.Q. Change." *Psychological Monographs* 77, No. 571 (1963).

(62) Hamburg, D. A., and Lunde, D. T. "Sex Hormones in the Development of Sex Differences in Human Behavior." In E. E. Maccoby (ed.), *The Development of Sex Differences.* Stanford, Calif.: Stanford University Press, 1966 pp. 1-24.

(63) Harlan, L. R. *Separate and Unequal.* New York: Atheneum Press, 1969.

(64) Harmatz, M. G. "Effects of Anxiety, Motivating Instructions, Success and Failure Reports, and Sex of Subject Upon Level of Aspiration and Performance." Unpublished master's thesis, University of Washington, 1962.

(65) Harris, A. S. "The Second Sex in Academe." *AAUP Bulletin* 56 (1970): 283-295.

(66) Hearings on Section 805 of H. R. 10698 before the Special Subcommittee on Education of the House Committee on Education and Labor, 91st Congress, 2nd Session, 1970.

(67) Horner, M. "Fail: Bright Women." *Psychology Today* 3 (November 1969): 36-38, 62.

(68) Howe, F. "Identity and Expression: A Writing Course for Women." Unpublished manuscript, Goucher College, July 1970.

(69) Hsia, J. *Integration in Evanston, 1967-71: A Longitudinal Evaluation* (PR-71-9). Princeton, N. J.: Educational Testing Service, August 1971.

(70) Hunnicut, C. W. et al. *We Play.* New York: Random House, Singer School Division, 1963.

(71) Hurley, J. F. "Report of Project Evaluation: Instructional Grouping by Sex at the Fifth Grade Level—A Study of All-Boy and All-Girl Groups." Office of Psychological Services, Fairfax County School Board, Fairfax, Virginia 22024, 1964.

(72) Hurley, J. F. "Report of Project Evaluations: A Study of All-Boy and All-Girl Groups at the Third and Fifth Grade Levels and an Evaluation after Two Years in Same Sex Classes." Office of Psychological Services, Fairfax County School Board, Fairfax, Virginia 22024, 1965.

(73) Iscoe, I., and Carden, J. A. "Field Dependence, Manifest Anxiety, and Sociometric Status in Children." *Journal of Consulting Psychology,* 25 (1961): 184.

(74) Jackson, P. W. *Life in Classrooms.* New York: Holt, Rinehart, and Winston, 1968.

(75) Jersild, A. T., and Holmes, F. B. "Children's Fears." *Child Development Monographs* No. 20 (1935): 1-356.

(76) Kagan, J. "The Child's Sex Role Classification of School Objects." *Child Development* 35 (1964): 1051-1056.

(77) Kagan, J. "Acquisition and Significance of Sex Typing and Sex Role Identity." In M. L. Hoffman and L. W. Hoffman (eds.), *Review of Child Development Research,* Vol. 1. New York: Russell Sage Foundation, 1964, pp. 137-167.

(78) Kagan, J., and Lewis, M. "Studies of Attention in the Human Infant." *Merrill-Palmer Quarterly* 11 (1965): 95-127.

(79) Kagan, J., and Moss, H. A. *Birth to Maturity.* New York: Wiley, 1962.

(80) Kagan, J.; Moss, H. A.; and Sigel, I. E. "The Psychological Significance of Styles of Conceptualization." In J. C. Wright and J. Kagan (eds.), *Basic*

Cognitive Processes in Children. Monographs of the Society for Research in Child Development 28, No. 2 (1963): 73-124.

(81) Kagan, J.; Rosman, B. L.; Day, D.; Phillips, A. J.; and Phillips, W. "Information Processing in the Child: Significance of Analytic and Reflective Attitudes." *Psychological Monographs* 78, No. 1 (1964).

(82) Kahne, H. "Women in the Professions: Career Consideration and Job Placement Techniques." *Journal of Economic Issues* 5, No. 3 (1971): 28-45.

(83) Katz, M. *The Irony of Early School Reform.* Cambridge, Mass.: Harvard University Press, 1968.

(84) Keezer, D. M. "Watch Out Girls!" *New Republic* 161 (Sept. 13, 1969): 30-31.

(85) Klausmeier, H. J., and Wiersma, W. "Relationship of Sex, Grade Level, and Locale to Performance of High I.Q. Students on Divergent Thinking Tests." *Journal of Educational Psychology* 55 (1964): 114-119.

(86) Kohlberg, L. "A Cognitive-Developmental Analysis of Children's Sex-Role Concepts and Attitudes." In E. E. Maccoby (ed.), *The Development of Sex Differences.* Stanford, Calif.: Stanford University Press, 1966, pp. 82-173.

(87) Leiderman, P. H., and Shapiro, D. "A Physiological and Behavioral Approach to the Study of Group Interaction." *Psychosomatic Medicine* 25 (1963): 146-157.

(88) Lewis, E. C. *Developing Woman's Potential.* Ames, Iowa: Iowa State University Press, 1968.

(89) Lieberman, M. *Education as a Profession.* Englewood Cliffs, N. J.: Prentice-Hall, 1956.

(90) Lovejoy, C. E. *Lovejoy's College Guide.* New York: Simon and Schuster, 1968.

(91) Maccoby, E. E. "Woman's Intellect." In S. M. Farber and R. L. Wilson (eds.), *The Potential of Woman.* New York: McGraw-Hill, 1963.

(92) Maccoby, E. E. "Sex Differences in Intellectual Functioning." In E. E. Maccoby (ed.), *The Development of Sex Differences.* Stanford, Calif.: Stanford University Press, 1966, pp. 25-55.

(93) Maccoby, E. E.; Dowley, E. M.; Degerman, J. W.; and Degerman, R. "Activity Level and Intellectual Functioning in Normal Preschool Children." *Child Development* 36 (1965): 761-770.

(94) Maccoby, E. E.; Hagen, J. N.; Sontag, L. W.; and Kagan, J. Unpublished report, Laboratory of Human Development, Stanford University, 1963.

(95) Maccoby, E. E., and Jacklin, C. N. "Sex Differences and Their Implication for Sex Roles." Paper presented at the American Psychological Association, Washington, D. C., 1971.

(96) Maccoby, E. E., and Rau, L. "Differential Cognitive Abilities." Final report, cooperative research project No. 1040, Stanford University, 1962.

(97) MacKinnon, D. W. "The Nature and Nurture of Creative Talent." *American Psychologist* 17 (1962): 484-495.

(98) Mason, W. S.; Dressel, R. S.; and Bain, R. K. "Sex Role and the Career Orientations of Beginning Teachers." *Harvard Educational Review* 29 (1959): 370-383.

(99) McCandless, B.; Bilous, C.; and Bennett, H. "Peer Popularity and Dependence on Adults in Preschool Socialization." *Child Development* 32 (1961): 511-518.

(100) McCarthy, D. "Language Development in Children." In L. Carmichael (ed.), *Manual of Child Psychology.* New York: Wiley, 1954, pp. 492-630.

(101) McClelland, D.; Atkinson, J. W.; Clark, R. A.; and Lowell, E. L. *The Achievement Motive.* New York: Appleton-Century-Crofts, 1953.

(102) McNeil, J. D. "Programed Instruction Versus Usual Classroom Procedures in Teaching Boys to Read." *American Educational Research Journal* 1 (1964): 113-119.

(103) Merriam, E. *Mommies at Work.* New York: Knopf, 1961.

(104) Meyer, W. J., and Thompson, G. G. "Sex Differences in the Distribution of Teacher Approval and Disapproval Among Sixth Grade Children." *Journal of Educational Psychology* 47 (1956): 385-396.

(105) Mill, J. S. *The Subjection of Women.* London: Oxford University Press, 1912 (first published in 1869).

(106) Millett, K. *Sexual Politics.* Garden City, N. Y.: Doubleday, 1970.

(107) Minuchin, P. "Sex Role Concepts and Sex Typing in Childhood as a Function of School and Home Environments." Paper presented at American Orthopsychiatric Association, Chicago, 1964.

(108) Mischel, W. "A Social-Learning View of Sex Differences in Behavior." In E. E. Maccoby (ed.), *The Development of Sex Differences*. Stanford, Calif.: Stanford University Press, 1966, pp. 56-81.

(109) Mischel, W. "Sex-Typing and Socialization." In P. H. Mussen (ed.), *Carmichael's Manual of Child Psychology* (3rd ed.), Vol. 2. New York: Wiley, 1970, pp. 3-72.

(110) Moss, H. A. "Sex, Age, and State as Determinants of Mother-Infant Interaction." *Merrill-Palmer Quarterly* 13 (1967): 19-36.

(111) Moss, H. A., and Kagan, J. Unpublished manuscript, 1962.

(112) Murray, P. "Economic and Educational Inequality Based on Sex: An Overview." *Valparaiso University Law Review* 5 (1971): 261.

(113) Mussen, P. H. "Early Sex-Role Development." In D. A. Goslin (ed.), *Handbook of Socialization Theory and Research*. Chicago: Rand McNally, 1969, pp. 707-731.

(114) Neugarten, B. L. "Women in a University." *School Review* 79 (1970): 109-114.

(115) Newcomber, M. *A Century of Higher Education for Women*. New York: Harper & Bros., 1958.

(116) Oetzel, R. "The Relationship Between Sex Role Acceptance and Cognitive Abilities." Unpublished master's thesis, Stanford University, 1961.

(117) Parrish, J. B. "Top Level Training of Women in the United States 1900-1960." *National Association of Women Deans and Counselors Journal* 25 (1962): 67-73.

(118) Phillips, B. N.; Hindsman, E.; and McGuire, C. "Factors Associated with Anxiety and Their Relation to the School Achievement of Adolescents." *Psychological Reports* 7 (1960): 365-372.

(119) Radcliffe Committee on Graduate Education for Women. *Graduate Education for Women*. Cambridge: Harvard University Press, 1956.

(120) Rau, L. "Interpersonal Correlates of Perceptual-Cognitive Functions." Paper presented at Society for Research in Child Development, San Francisco, 1963.

(121) Reimer, E. *School is Dead: Alternatives in Education*. Garden City, N. Y.: Doubleday, 1971.

(122) Reynolds, M. *The Learned Lady in England 1650-1760*. Boston: Houghton Mifflin, 1920.

(123) Rosenthal, A. *Pedagogues and Power: Teacher Groups in School Politics*. Syracuse, New York: Syracuse University Press, 1969.

(124) Rosenthal, R., and Jacobson, L. *Pygmalion in the Classroom*. New York: Holt, Rinehart and Winston, 1968.

(125) Rosenthal, R., and Rubin, D. B. "Pygmalion Reaffirmed." In J. D. Elashoff and R. E. Snow, *Pygmalion Reconsidered*. Worthington, Ohio: Charles A. Jones, 1971, pp. 139-155.

(126) Rossi, A. S. "Discrimination and Demography Restrict Opportunities for Academic Women." *College and University Business* 48 (February, 1970): 74-78.

(127) Rossi, A. S. "The Status of Women in Graduate Departments of Sociology: 1968-69." *American Sociologist* 5, No. 1 (1970).

(128) Rush, B. "Thoughts Upon Female Education, Accommodated to the Present State of Society, Manners, and Government in the United States of America" (Boston, 1787). Reprinted in F. Rudolph (ed.), *Essays on Education in the Early Republic*. Cambridge, Mass.: Harvard University Press, 1965, pp. 26-40.

(129) Russell, D. G., and Sarason, E. G. "Test Anxiety, Sex, and Experimental Conditions in Relation to Anagram Solution." *Journal of Personality and Social Psychology* 1 (1965): 493-496.

(130) Scheffe', H. *The Analysis of Variance*. New York: Wiley, 1959.

(131) Sears, P. S. *The Effect of Classroom Conditions on the Strength of Achievement Motive and Work Output on Elementary School Children*. Final report, Cooperative Research Project No. 873, Stanford University, 1963.

(132) Seashore, H. G. "Women are More Predictable Than Men." *Journal of Counseling Psychology* 9 (1962): 261-270.

(133) Sexton, P. *The Feminized Male*. New York: Random House, 1969.

(134) Shaw, M. C., and McCuen, J. T. "The Onset of Academic Underachievement in Bright Children." *Journal of Educational Psychology* 51 (1960): 103-108.

(135) Sigel, I. "Sex Differences in Cognitive Functioning Reexamined: A Functional Point of View." Paper presented at Society for Research in Child Development, Berkeley, California, 1964.

(136) Sigel, I.; Jarman, P.; and Hanesian, H. "Styles of Categorization and Their Perceptual, Intellectual, and Personality Correlates in Young Children." Unpublished paper, Merrill-Palmer Institute, 1963.

(137) Silberman, C. E. *Crisis in the Classroom: The Remaking of American Education.* New York: Random House, 1970.

(138) Simpson, L. A. "A Study of Employing Agents' Attitudes Toward Academic Women in Higher Education." Doctoral dissertation, Pennsylvania State University, 1968.

(139) Sontag, L. W. "Physiological Factors and Personality in Children." *Child Development* 18 (1947): 185-189.

(140) Sontag, L. W.; Baker, C. T.; and Nelson, V. A. "Mental Growth and Personality Development: A Longitudinal Study." *Monographs of the Society for Research in Child Development* 23, No. 68 (1958).

(141) Stanley, J. C. "Further Evidence Via the Analysis of Variance That Women Are More Predictable Academically Than Men." *Ontario Journal of Educational Research* 10 (1967): 49-56.

(142) Stanley, J. C., and Porter, A. C. "Correlation of Scholastic Aptitude Test Scores With College Grades for Negroes vs. Whites." *Journal of Educational Measurement* 4 (1967): 199-218.

(143) Steinem, G. "What It Would Be Like if Women Win." *Time,* Aug. 31, 1970. Reprinted in *Liberation Now!* New York: Dell, 1971, pp. 55-61.

(144) Strickler, R. W. "Thomas Coeburn Elementary School Kindergarten-Primary Masculinization Project 1968-1972 and Kindergarten-Primary Masculinization Project 1970-71." Unpublished manuscripts, Penn-Delco School District, 95 Concord Road, Aston, Pa., 19014.

(145) Swift, J. A Letter to a Very Young Lady on Her Marriage. In *Miscellanies,* 1727. Reprinted in Temple Scott (ed.), *The Prose Works of Jonathan Swift.* Vol. XI Literary Essays. London: George Bell, 1907, pp. 115-124.

(146) Tanner, J. M. "Physical Growth." In P. H. Mussen (ed.), *Carmichael's Manual of Child Psychology,* Vol. I. New York: Wiley, 1970, pp. 77-155.

(147) Taylor, J. A., and Spence, K. W. "The Relationship of Anxiety Level to Performance in Serial Learning." *Journal of Experimental Psychology* 44 (1952): 61-64.

(148) Terman, L. M., and Oden, M. H. *The Gifted Child Grows Up.* Stanford. Calif. Stanford University Press, 1947.

(149) Terman, L. M., and Tyler, L. E. "Psychological Sex Differences." In L. Carmichael (ed.), *Manual of Child Psychology* (2nd ed.). New York: Wiley, 1954.

(150) Thomas, M. C. "Should the Higher Education of Women Differ From That of Men?" *Educational Review* 21 (1901): 1-10. Reprinted (abridged) in B. M. Cross (ed.), *The Educated Woman in America.* New York: Teachers College Press, 1965, pp. 145-154.

(151) Trembly, D. "Age and Sex Differences in Creative Thinking Potential." Paper presented at the American Psychological Association, Los Angeles, 1964.

(152) Tulkin, S. R.; Muller, J. P.; and Conn, L. K. "Need for Approval and Popularity: Sex Differences in Elementary School Students." *Journal of Consulting Psychology* 33 (1969): 35-39.

(153) Tyler, L. E. "A Comparison of the Interests of English and American School Children." *Journal of Genetic Psychology* 88 (1956): 175-181.

(154) Tyler, L. E. "Individual Differences: Sex Differences." In D. L. Sills (ed.), *International Encyclopedia of the Social Sciences,* Vol. 7. New York: Macmillan Co. & The Free Press, 1968, pp. 207-213.

(155) Waller, W. *The Sociology of Teaching.* New York: Russell and Russell, 1961.

(156) Walster, E.; Cleary, T. A.; and Clifford, M. M. "The Effect of Race and Sex on College Admission." *Sociology of Education* 44 (1971): 237-244.

(157) Walster, G. W., and Cleary, T. A. "The Use of Statistical Significance as a Decision Rule." In E. F. Borgatta and G. W. Bohrnstedt (eds.), *Sociological Methodology 1970,* Vol. 2. San Francisco: Jossey-Bass, 1970, pp. 246-254.

(158) Walter, D.; Denzler, L. S.; and Sarason, E. G. "Anxiety and the Intellectual Performance of High School Students." *Child Development* 35 (1964): 917-926.

(159) *What Teachers Think: A Summary of Teacher Opinion Poll Findings,* 1960-1965. Washington, D. C.: National Education Association–Research Division, September 1965. Research Report 1965-R 13.

(160) Williams, R. C. "Teacher Militancy: Implications for the Schools." In P. Piele and T. Eidell (eds.), *Social and Technological Change.* Eugene, Oregon: University of Oregon Press, 1970.

(161) Wisenthal, M. "Sex Differences in Attitudes and Attainment in Junior Schools." *British Journal of Educational Psychology* 35 (1965): 79-85.

(162) Witkin, H. A. "Social Influences in the Development of Cognitive Style." In D. A. Goslin (ed.), *Handbook of Socialization Theory and Research.* Chicago: Rand McNally, 1969, pp. 687-706.

(163) Witkin, H. A.; Dyk, R. B.; Faterson, H. F.; Goodenough, D. R.; and Karp, S. A. *Psychological Differentiation.* New York: Wiley, 1962.

(164) Witkin, H. A.; Lewis, H. B.; Herzman, M.; Machover, K.; Meissner, P. B.; and Wapner, S. *Personality Through Perception.* New York: Harper, 1954.

(165) Women on Words and Images. *Dick and Jane as Victims: Sex Stereotyping in Children's Readers,* 1971. Report available from 25 Cleveland Lane, R D #4, Princeton, N. J. 08540.

(166) Woolf, V. *A Room of One's Own.* New York: Harcourt, Brace, 1929.

The Charles A. Jones Publishing Company

International Series in Education

Adams, *Simulation Games*

Allen, Barnes, Reece, Roberson, *Teacher Self-Appraisal: A Way of Looking Over Your Own Shoulder*

Armstrong, Cornell, Kraner, Roberson, *The Development and Evaluation of Behavioral Objectives*

Braun, Edwards, *History and Theory of Early Childhood Education*

Carlton, Goodwin, *The Collective Dilemma: Negotiations in Education*

Criscuolo, *Improving Classroom Reading Instruction*

Crosswhite, Higgins, Osborne, Shumway, *Mathematics Teaching: Psychological Foundations*

Denues, *Career Perspective: Your Choice of Work*

DeStefano, *Language, Society, and Education: A Profile of Black English*

Doll, *Leadership to Improve Schools*

Drier, *K-12 Guide for Integrating Career Development into Local Curriculum*

Foster, Fitzgerald, Beal, *Career Education and Vocational Guidance*

Frymier, Hawn, *Curriculum Improvement for Better Schools*

Goodlad, Klein, Associates, *Behind the Classroom Door*

Hauenstein, *Curriculum Planning for Behavioral Development*

Higgins, *Mathematics Teaching and Learning*

Hitt, *Education as a Human Enterprise*

Leland, Smith, *Mental Retardation: Perspectives for the Future*

Lutz, *Toward Improved Urban Education*

Meyer, *A Statistical Analysis of Behavior*

National Society for the Study of Education, *Contemporary Educational Issues* (10 book series)

Nerbovig, *Unit Planning: A Model for Curriculum Development*

Overly, Kinghorn, Preston, *The Middle School: Humanizing Education for Youth*

Perry, Wildman, *The Impact of Negotiations in Public Education: The Evidence from the Schools*

Poston, *Implementing Career Education*

Pula, Goff, *Technology in Education: Challenge and Change*

Ressler, *Career Education: The New Frontier*

Rich, *Humanistic Foundations of Education*

Shane, Shane, Gibson, Munger, *Guiding Human Development: The Counselor and the Teacher in the Elementary School*

Swanson, *Evaluation in Education*

Thiagarajan, *The Programing Process: A Practical Guide*

Von Haden, King, *Innovations in Education: Their Pros and Cons*

Weber, *Early Childhood Education: Perspectives on Change*

Wernick, *Career Education in the Elementary School*

Wiles, *Changing Perspectives in Educational Research*

Wiman, *Instructional Materials*

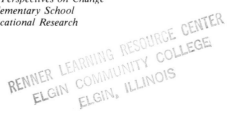